THE DIVINE COUNTRY

The
Divine Country

The British in Tuscany

1372 – 1980

=

OLIVE HAMILTON

You cannot conceive what a divine
country this is just now; the vines
with their young leaves hang as if
they were of thin beaten gold—
everywhere—the bright green of the
young corn sets off the grey purple
of the olive hills, and the spring skies
have been every one backgrounds of
Fra Angelico.

JOHN RUSKIN, 3 May 1845 to his father

ANDRE DEUTSCH

First published 1982 by
André Deutsch Limited
105 Great Russell Street London WC1

ISBN 0 233 97425 3

Typeset by Gloucester Typesetting Services

Printed in Great Britain by
Ebenezer Baylis Limited
The Trinity Press,
Worcester, and London

For
Michael, Nigel,
Adrian and John

Contents

LIST OF ILLUSTRATIONS

Acknowledgements

I am grateful to many people for their help, and especially for the practical assistance of the late Mr James Dow, and to Signora Giuliana Artom Treves who read the manuscript to check my Italian; also to: Sir Harold Acton; Miss C. J. Baker; the late Prince T. Corsini; Professor Rosemary Cramp; Major Greville Cripps; Mrs J. Dow; Mr Alastair Dunnett; Mr John Fleming (on whose articles about the Hugfords of Florence I have leaned heavily); Mrs Trevor Fenwick; Mr John P. Fuller; Mr John Gere; Mr Ian Greenlees; Mr Robert Harling; Lt.Col. Kenneth Henderson; Professor Max Jaffé; Dr Hanna Kiel; Mr Donald King; Mr J. W. Lambert; Signor G. G. Natalicchi, London representative of Monte dei Paschi di Siena; the late General Sir Richard O'Connor; Professor Giuliano Pellegrini; Mr John Physick; Sir John Pope-Hennessy; Mrs John Primavesi; Mr Denys Sutton; Mr John Walker; Mr Andrew Wilton.

Thanks are due to the following for permission to reproduce: The Trustees of the British Museum for 'The Rigours of the Road'; The British Library Reference Division for 'Geoffrey Chaucer as portrayed in *De Regimine Principium*'; Edizione Alinari and the Mansell Collection for 'Aeneas Silvius Piccolomini being received by James I', for the detail from the cope of Pope Pius II and for Canova's monument to the Stuarts; The Monte dei Paschi di Siena bank for 'The hall of Salimbeni Castle'; The Trustees of the Scottish National Gallery for the portrait of Charles Edward Stuart; Her Majesty the Queen for gracious permission to reproduce a detail from Zoffany's 'The Tribuna'; The Director of the Victoria and Albert Museum for the bust of Dr Cocchi; The President of St John's College, Oxford, for Gori's portrait of Enrico Hugford; The Trustees of

Acknowledgements

the National Portrait Gallery for the portraits of Maria Clementina Sobieska, Robert Adam and John Ruskin; The Rector of the University of Florence and the Dean of the Faculty of Architecture for the fresco of the Royal Arms of England on a wall of the Palazzo Guadagni (now Clemente); The Ashmolean Museum, Oxford, for Ruskin's drawing of San Martino, Lucca.

O.H.

Preface

WHEN I wrote *Paradise of Exiles* (André Deutsch, 1974) I felt that I had done not nearly enough to cover the subject of the very strong British–Tuscan connection. The interest aroused by that first and scarcely adequate effort has led me to this second attempt to do justice, in a purely personal way, to the Tuscan influence on the British.

That influence is as powerful today as ever, not least in my own life. It is now a good many years since we first put down some of our roots in Tuscany, but we still feel a suppressed excitement whenever we approach Pisa from the air. Driving towards the Carrara mountains with their summits sprinkled with marble dust, and the peaks of the Apuan Alps beyond, we arrive finally at the gracious tree-lined avenues approaching the old town which lies in the valley below our house, then climb past the ancient church and up the steep road amid the olives, to the welcoming faces that await us.

The most obvious change in the daily life of our valley in recent years has been the arrival of the piped water to every house. This has been an enormous help in the cultivation of the land and has eased the burden on the women. The voices from the communal washing cisterns no longer echo across the valley, alas, as they have done for centuries; but if one no longer sees bowls of laundry borne on the heads of erect and stately figures, the shopping is still carried this way up the mountain road.

The young today all seem to have motor cars or motor scooters, but they still attend the local religious festivals with their colourful processions. Recently I was able to take part for the first time in the Festival of the Cross at Lucca. The late September evening was warm, the air soft. After attending vespers in the Duomo, conducted by the Bishop, and examining at close range the magnificent early crucifix, the Volto Santo, the elegant ironwork gates of Civitali's grille having been opened for the occasion, we sat amid the chattering throng of Lucchese in the busy square of San Michele.

Here all artificial lighting was extinguished and the glow of candles and oil lamps flickered on the sides of the huge church and in the streets around. Through the square wound the procession, the crucifix representing the Volto Santo carried aloft, followed by groups bearing the banners of the different parts of the province, accompanied of course by a band. The pretty young girl selling candy-floss near my chair was just packing up, and with typical kindliness ushered me to a position in the crowd from which I could see everything as the procession wove its way along the Via Filolungo, from the church of San Frediano to the cathedral church of San Martino.

Other cities of Tuscany—Florence, Siena, Arezzo, Pisa, Pistoia, Volterra and Carrara—are still magnets for us. But for Lucca we feel, as Augustus Hare wrote in 1896 to Lord Halifax,

Oh! the difference . . . on finding oneself in the delightful old-world streets of Lucca, with their clean pavements and brown green-shuttered houses, with the air so much more bracing, the sky so much more soft, and the pleasant manner and winning tongue of the Italian people.

O.H.
London 1981

The Rigours of
Travel

THERE were several different routes from England to Tuscany
in the fourteenth century, when Geoffrey Chaucer first made the
journey, and all of them were difficult. The traveller had first to
brave the Channel crossing, which in bad weather could take
eleven days. French privateers infested the offshore waters, but
these were less to be feared than the wild mountain people in the
Alpine passes, who would, it was said, slit a man's throat for no
more than the silver he could carry in his money belt. The overland route was through France and over the Mont-Cenis pass, or
through Germany and over the Brenner, depending on which
country was likely to be less hostile to a travelling Englishman;
a route not so often used was via Basle and Lucerne and over the
St Gotthard—this last being judged 'a perilous passage where
snow waters thundered like the sea and mules were buried in
snow'.[1] And having got over the Alps and down to the coast
at Genoa, say, the traveller had still to go on to Florence over
what Dante described as the 'most desolate and solitary way' that
lies between Lerici and Turbia.[2]

The astonishing thing is how many Englishmen made this
perilous journey across Europe, on foot or on horseback. At first
the travellers were mainly monks, going as pilgrims to Rome by
way of Tuscany. In the seventh century Benedict Biscop,
founder in 674 and 682 of the Monkwearmouth and Jarrow
monasteries, journeyed to Rome six times. On one occasion he
was accompanied by Ceolfrith, teacher of the Venerable Bede.
When the same Ceolfrith decided in old age to make a last
pilgrimage to Rome, he took with him as a gift for the Pope one

---

[1] BL: Sloane MS 682, fo. 8.   [2] *Purgatorio*, III, 49.

of the three great Bibles he had had copied and illuminated in the scriptorium of his monastery. The enormous codex of 2,060 calfskin pages, weighing with its covers some ninety pounds, was borne by a retinue of eighty monks. The journey proved too much for Ceolfrith, who died on the way at the monastery of Langres in France, but some of the monks went on to Rome with his magnificent gift. Known as the Codex Amiatinus, this Bible, the only one of the three made at Jarrow to have been preserved, is now in the Laurentian Library in Florence.

In the early Middle Ages, studious (and sturdy) English monks crossed the Alps in search of enlightenment, and to study manuscripts of which no copies were available at home. Church dignitaries from England also made the journey, just as Vatican officials on the Pope's business travelled in the opposite direction; but they had horses to bear their ponderous dignity and swordsmen to protect them. Merchants, too, travelled to Tuscany, with mules laden with English wool for the great clothing trade of Florence, finding inns along the way and a palliasse for a night's rest.

It is not known by which route Geoffrey Chaucer, our own poetic genius, travelled to Genoa in 1372, when he went there on diplomatic business for Edward III, but we know in some detail what he did when he got there. He was at the time in the service of the Duke of Gloucester, whom he had discreetly made the hero of his first narrative poem, *The Boke of the Duchesse* (1369), and was described as 'one of the King's esquires'. In Genoa he was to make arrangements with the Doge and his merchants for the reopening of sea trade with England. They had to agree upon an English port that would not expose the Genoese to too many dangers, and probably Southampton was chosen: some of the finest houses in Bugle Street and French Street in that city are known to have belonged to Genoese and Venetian merchants. Chaucer then went on to Florence.

In 1372 Giovanni Boccaccio was fifty-nine; Chaucer was thirty-two. The Englishman had produced the first of his *Canterbury Tales* about 1364; the *Decameron* of Boccaccio was completed in 1348. There is some likelihood that Chaucer had heard of Boccaccio when he arrived in Genoa. He would undoubtedly have heard of Dante, who had been dead fifty years and whose fame had spread even to England: some monks who had travelled there from Italy could recite all thirty-four cantos of the *Inferno* before supper and most of the *Purgatorio* after. Chaucer had unquestionably heard of Petrarch, the greatest living Italian writer of this time, for it was from or through Petrarch, then in Padua, that the author of the *Canterbury Tales* got the translation (into Latin) of Boccaccio's tale of 'Griselda', which was to inspire his own *Clerk's Tale*. In the poem he notes that it was

> At Padowe of a worthy clerk
> As proved by his words and his work . . .
> Fraunces Petrark, the laureat poet
> Highte this clerk whose rhetorique swete . . .[3]

But Petrarch was Boccaccio's friend, and had helped to further his career. He had sent Boccaccio a copy of the Latin 'Griselda', so it may well have been in Florence, and from the author of the *Decameron* himself, that Chaucer got the translation, without having to climb any more mountains.

Chaucer makes no mention anywhere in his writings of Boccaccio. Yet he can scarcely have been in Florence in August 1373 without going to hear Boccaccio deliver his first discourse from the Chair for the Exposition of Dante's *Divina Commedia,* to which he had just been appointed by the Signoria. Chaucer had by then read or learned enough to have a strong curiosity about this Florentine whose works were to have such an influence on him. The two would have had much to talk about, no doubt in halting Latin—as, in the centuries that followed, many British visitors were laboriously to fight their way through the language barrier in order to comprehend and assimilate the artistic genius of Florence.

The meeting in August of 1373, if indeed it took place, was not to be repeated. Boccaccio died two years later, and Chaucer on his return to England became Comptroller of the Customs and Subsidies of Wools, Skins and Tanned Hides in the Port of

---

[3] Sir Harris Nicolas, *Life of Geoffrey Chaucer* (1810).

London. The job left him little time to devote to his tales; he even had to keep the customs records in his own hand. But his dealings with the Tuscan creditors of the King were made easier by his having visited Italy, and in the work he did manage to do between 1374 and 1386 there is evidence of a strong Italian influence. His *Troylus and Cryseyde* was based on Boccaccio's *Filostrato*, and *The Knight's Tale* in the *Canterbury Tales* on his *Teseida*; Chaucer also followed the overall design of Boccaccio's *Decameron* in the *Canterbury Tales*, and *The Parlement of Foules* and *The Hous of Fame*, though composed in his own unmistakable style and with their roots firmly in his native land, owe much to his Tuscan connection.

Chaucer wrote for a small sophisticated audience, members of the Court and a few cultured outsiders, to whom he read his work aloud before the poems were circulated in manuscript among the city and country gentry. Alas, none of these manuscripts survive; but we do know how Chaucer looked at this period—plump, with grey hair and a pointed beard, wearing a black hood and a calm serious expression—from the miniature portrait of him in *De Regimine Principium* (1411–12),[4] a work by his friend and disciple Thomas Hoccleve.

In 1378, Chaucer was sent on another diplomatic mission to Italy—this time to Milan, with Sir Edward Berkeley. They were to negotiate secretly with the Milanese ruler, Bernabo Visconti, and with the great English mercenary soldier, Sir John Hawkwood, who the previous year had married Visconti's illegitimate daughter, the beautiful Donnina. Chaucer remained fascinated by Visconti, whose death in 1385 he recounted in *The Monk's Tale*. He spent the whole summer of 1378 in northern Italy, and his total expenses were £80—a large sum then; no doubt it covered the purchase of manuscripts, so that at home again in England he could add to his knowledge of Italian literature.

After Chaucer's visits there is a gap in the record of Italian cultural influence in Britain until another Duke of Gloucester, Humphrey, son of Henry IV, appears on the scene. Duke

---

[4] BM Harleian MS 4866, fo. 91.

4

Humphrey's gifts to the University of Oxford, in 1437 and succeeding years, of copies of manuscripts which formed the nucleus
of what is now the Bodleian Library, stimulated the study of the
classics, of which the British until then had had only a meagre
knowledge. But it was not until much later that any great
number of British students in search of classical, or what came to
be called 'humanistic' learning began to make their way to
Italian universities. And when they did there were obvious
dangers, moral and intellectual as well as physical, in the journey.
For the new doctrine of humanism, based on the teachings of the
Greek philosophers, was far from acceptable to the Church: to
the learned clerics of the Curia in Rome, it represented a denial
of the Church's absolute authority over man's thought. At such
a time it took courage to defy the Establishment, as we would
call it, in order to respond to the new ideas.

How many British students went to Italian universities is
impossible to establish, for the records kept at that time were
sadly inadequate. At Siena, for instance, Englishmen or Scots
attending the University were listed as '*Tedeschi*' (Germans). If a
student fell into debt after reaching Siena, as was frequently the
case, he had to beg for food or do odd jobs as a not very useful
labourer. And if he was unlucky enough to die there he was
interred unceremoniously at the church of San Domenico, his
burial recorded as '*Theutonicus*'.[5] One such student, buried at
Siena in 1481, was more amply described, it is true, as Eduardus
Anglicus, the English Edward. After crossing the Alps, and facing
unknown hazards in his quest for knowledge, poor Edward,
whoever he was, had perhaps had to wait too long for money
from home to discharge his debts and to pay for his degree. That
beautifully inscribed *laurea* was one of the most expensive items
in a university career, for the professors had to be plied with
gifts—embroidered gloves and other offerings, as well as sums of
money—when the degree was awarded.

Several outstanding Englishmen braved the displeasure of the
Church and the perils of the journey to discover the new learning and to bring it to England in the fifteenth century. One of the

[5] Obituario di San Domenico, now in Biblioteca Comunale, Siena: MS C,
III.2.

first of these was Andrew Ols (his name may possibly have been Ellis), who was sent as a royal envoy to the Pope, and spent some time in Florence. Whilst having manuscripts copied there, he was welcomed into the circle of the ruler, Lorenzo de' Medici. This was Lorenzo the Magnificent, who took over from Piero the Gouty in 1449. Ols or Ellis must have impressed that circle, which gave the Renaissance its great impetus, for he was the subject of a biography written in Italian by Vespasiano da Bisticci. Vespasiano said of Ols that few foreigners could match his culture, and also noted obliquely that the Englishman had abandoned his native habit of remaining several hours at table for 'the more sober Italian manner of living'. During his stay in Italy Ols had so many manuscripts copied that he could not send the copies overland, but had to wait for a ship sailing for England from Leghorn.

After Ols there came William Grey, Bishop of Ely, a generous and discerning patron, travelling with a noble's escort; John Free with only ten pounds in his purse; William Grocyn, already a man of forty, and his friend Thomas Linacre, a leading physician, who on their return were to be the teachers of More, Colet and Erasmus—these and many more of the early humanists made the journey to Tuscany and beyond.

Another great collector of Italian manuscripts at this time was the cruel but cultivated John Tiptoft, Earl of Worcester, who was Lord Treasurer and a Privy Councillor under Henry VI. Tiptoft's father had helped the Lancastrian Henry to the throne; on the other hand, the Worcesters were related by birth to the Yorkists and by ties of friendship to the Nevilles, the stoutest allies of York. After Henry was deposed, Tiptoft found it a convenient time to make a pilgrimage to the Holy Land, and was wise enough to stop off in Italy on the way back, to await better news from home.

He was in Padua in 1461, for there is a reference to him, as 'il conte Giovanni inglese' (the English Count John) in the Medici letters of that year.[6] He was an ambitious student as well as a politician, and when Giovanni de' Medici invited him to Florence, where he could meet the leading humanists and artists,

[6] Archivio di Stato, Florence: Medici avanti principati filza 10, n 7.

Tiptoft accepted, taking with him his 'great store of books'. In Florence he was soon slipping in to the University, dressed soberly and unattended, to mingle with the crowds of students who went to hear the lively, provocative morning lectures of Argiropoulos, the foremost Greek scholar in Italy at the time. Tiptoft was also gathering more and more copies of manuscripts —so many that he was said to have despoiled the libraries of Italy to enrich those of England—which were later presented to the University of Oxford. One of his most exciting finds was a copy of Lucretius' *De Rerum Natura*, a work quite unknown in England, by an author then little known even in Italy.

From Florence Tiptoft made his way to Rome, where his eloquence apparently moved Pope Pius II to tears, and finally back to England, to political power and to his destined end (he was executed in 1470), from which all his learning and service to Oxford could not save him. But his legacy of books did much to spread humanism in England.

English travellers to Italy in succeeding centuries recorded in greater detail their journeyings and the minutiae of Tuscan life. Fynes Moryson, son of Thomas Moryson, M.P. for Great Grimsby, left a lively and fresh account of his travels in 1591, when no aspect of daily life seems to have escaped his observant eye:

> The Florentines are of spare diet, but wonderful clenlinesse. Those of Lucca keepe good mediocritie in all things. The Tyberine Peares and Marioline cheeses are great dainties. Those of Genoa are of most spare diet, and no clenliness. . . . The Sinnennesi eat magnifically and their dainties are Goates flesh and fresh cheese. . . . The Italians generally compared with the English or French, are most sparing in their diet.[7]

Moryson was sure the Italians surpassed us also in the arrangement and furnishing of their gardens, designed with an eye to posterity, especially in the use of water, and their adornment with statues.

[7] This and following quotations from Moryson's *An Itinerary* (1617).

'In the State of Florence,' he wrote, 'and especially at Sienna, a stranger may live . . . more commodiously than in any other part of Italy, because the inhabitants are most courteous . . . and strangers need not stand in feare of being murthered, as in Lombardy they doe.' In Florence he was impressed by what he found in the inns, where

> . . . from morning to night the Tables are spread with white cloathes, strewed with flowers and figge leaves, with Ingestars or glasses of divers coloured wines set upon them, and delicate fruits; . . . At the table they touch no meat with the hand, but with a forke of silver or other metall each man being served with his forke and spoone, and glasses to drink. As they serve small peeces of flesh (not whole joints as with us) so these peeces are cut into small bits to be taken up with the forke, and they seeth the flesh it be very tender.

He gives detailed advice to the traveller on the procedure for examining the bed. Owing to the warmer climate there would be no feather beds but a hard mattress and clean sheets must be insisted on, he says, and if unobtainable then linen breeches should be worn, 'for the Italians if they have no kine of the French pox, yet for the most part are troubled with an itch.'

As a Protestant in a Catholic country, Moryson shared the fear of religious persecution prevalent at the time, which sometimes impelled him to put on a disguise. He tells an amusing story of another Englishman who had visited Rome disguised, for the same reason, as a Swiss. On his departure he was followed to Florence by a messenger from the Inquisition demanding his arrest. However, a friend at the Grand Duke's court warned him, and he

> presently tooke him to his heeles towards Paduoa, in such haste, as hee seemed to flie over the Appennine without wings. Anow (God be praised) hee is in safetie. . . . I cannot hold from laughing [said Moryson] when I imagin . . . what large steppes he makes over the rockey Mountains.

Another interesting traveller in Tuscany around the end of the sixteenth century was the outrageous Sir Henry Wotton, famous as the author of the witty, if indiscreet, description of an ambassador as 'an honest man sent to lie abroad for the good of his country' which was to land him in temporary disgrace at the court of James I.

Wotton had earlier won James's favour by his daring and enterprise as another kind of ambassador. He had been in Tuscany in the last decade of the century, apparently under orders from England to keep an eye on the court of the Florentine Grand Duke Ferdinand I, and he was back again in 1602 when Queen Elizabeth's health was failing and James VI of Scotland seemed assured of succeeding to her throne. In Florence Wotton and others got to know of a slightly mad Englishman living there, Humphrey Dethick, who was travelling to Scotland, as he later confessed, in order to kill the King. Belisario Venta, private secretary to the Grand Duke, was renowned for his knowledge of antidotes to poison, and Wotton, who had become friendly with Venta, was chosen by Ferdinand to carry a casket of these antidotes to James, with a dispatch 'of high and secret importance' about the succession to the English throne. As he spoke the language well, Wotton disguised himself as an Italian (an Englishman wouldn't have got far in Scotland), taking the name of Ottavio Baldi. Arriving in Dunfermline, he was taken to the King and after delivering his message in Italian, he leaned forward and whispered to James in English; when he revealed his identity, he was given a private audience. Apart from the importance of his mission, the idea of a young Englishman successfully masquerading as an Italian appealed to the King, and when James VI duly became James I of England Wotton was given advancement in his court at Winchester—at least until his witticism about ambassadors got round.

In Florence in 1610 the political philosopher Thomas Hobbes, making the Grand Tour as tutor to the Earl of Devonshire's heir, met and 'contracted a friendship' (as John Aubrey reports)

> with the famous Galileo Galilei, whom he extremely venerated and magnified; and not only as he was a prodigious witt, but for

his sweetness of nature and manners. They pretty well resembled one another as to their countenance as by their pictures doth appear; were both cheerful and melancholique-sanguine; and had both a consimilitie of Fate, to be hated and persecuted by Ecclesiastiques.[8]

In 1635 and 1636 Hobbes visited the scientist at his villa at Arcetri, and this obviously turned his mind to mathematics. Already a brilliant classical scholar, Hobbes now learned French and Italian, and through the latter came to the work of Machiavelli, also an important influence on his thinking.

Throughout the seventeenth century Englishmen in search of learning or art continued to make the rigorous journey to Italy. In 1613 Lord Arundel and Inigo Jones entered the country via the St Gotthard Pass to Lugano and Milan, but this route, as we have seen, had an evil reputation. Coming over the Alps into Italy in 1658, Francis Mortoft and his companions rode along dangerous mountain paths where the inhabitants crowded round, swearing and frightening them. From Genoa to Massa they observed that 'for some 60 Mile together' the mountains were 'al covered with Chestnutt Trees, whereof the People . . . makes Chestnut Bread, which suffices them instead of others'.

Mortoft's party continued some twenty-six miles to Lucca, which the Englishman thought

> one of the Prettyest contrivedst Cittyes in Italy and a free Common wealth, those of the Towne choosing a Duke every two Months, which they take and carry to the Pallace, where he is not suffered to speak with his wife and Children all the while of his government.[9]

Mortoft described the three gates of the city and the wall 'of the Breadth of two Coaches' which completely encircled it for two miles, and which provided the citizens with a much used walk on the ramparts.

Throughout the eighteenth century, even by the less dangerous

---

[8] *Aubrey's Brief Lives*, ed. Oliver Lawson Dick (1950).
[9] *Francis Mortoft, His Book* (1658).

route through France, over the Mont-Cenis and down to Turin, the journey to Italy remained arduous. When the poet Thomas Gray came this way with Horace Walpole, the Prime Minister's son, in the autumn of 1739, it took them six days in all, and Gray pictured them as 'as well armed as possible against the cold with muffs, hoods and masks of beaver, fur boots and bear skins'.[10]

Another eighteenth-century traveller, Samuel Sharpe, has a vivid account of crossing the Mont-Cenis:

> The passage into Italy is composed of a very steep ascent, almost three miles high; then of a plain, nearly flat, about five or six miles long; and lastly of a descent about six miles in length. . . . Both going and returning, when you arrive at the foot of the hill, your coach, or chaise, is taken to pieces and carried upon mules to the other side, and you yourself are transported by two men, on a common straw sedan chair, with a swinging foot-board to prop up your feet; but though it be the work of two men only to carry you, six and sometimes eight, attend, in order to relieve one another. The whole way that you ride in this manner being fourteen or fifteen miles, when the person carried is corpulent, it is necessary to employ ten porters.[11]

Montaigne in the sixteenth century had been carried by eight porters in relays of four, then descended by sledge.

The paths were narrow, steep and ice-covered in winter, and exposed to avalanches. Thomas Nugent gives an horrific description of the St Gotthard, where

> the most hazardous part is the bridge on the Russ, called the Bridge of Hell, from the horrid noise the water makes as it tumbles from the rocks, and from the slipperiness of the bridge, which renders it difficult even to foot passengers, who are obliged to creep on all-fours, lest the fury of the winds should drive them down the rocks.[12]

No wonder the ailing novelist Tobias Smollett preferred in 1765 to go via France to the Mediterranean:

[10] *Letters of Thomas Gray*, vol. II (1900).
[11] *Letters from Italy* (1756).
[12] *The Grand Tour* (1756).

Certainly no person who travels to Italy from England, Holland, France or Spain would make a troublesome circuit to pass the Alps by the way of Savoy and Piedmont, if he could have the convenience of the post by way of Aix, Antibes, and Nice along the side of the Mediterranean . . . which affords the most agreeable prospect I ever beheld.

Smollett travelled in an open boat, known as a felucca, from Nice to Genoa, 'rowed by ten or twelve' stout mariners. He explained that these boats, designed to carry passengers or cargo in coastal traffic, were

large enough to take in a post-chaise and there is a tilt over the stern where the passengers sit, to protect them from the rain; between the seats one person may lie commodiously on a mattrass supplied by the patron; A man in good health may put up with anything; but I would advise every valetudinarian who travels this way, to provide his own chaise, mattrass and bed linnen, otherwise he will pass his time very uncomfortably.[13]

One of the passengers travelling with him was feeling ill and begged to land at San Remo, where they stayed in a dirty and unpleasant inn. Owing to high winds they had to remain there until the third day when they re-embarked and eventually arrived at Genoa and found a good inn. Smollett had a pass signed by the British consul in Nice and letters of recommendation to the consuls at Genoa and Leghorn, and he strongly advised others to obtain the same in case of accidents on the road.

Many of those who travelled to Tuscany in the eighteenth century went out of their way to visit Lucca. This was not because of the architecture of its churches or its works of art; Lord Herbert of Cherbury, who arrived at the main gate of the city just before sunset in November 1779, allotted only one hour for 'the most curious of mortals to see the capital of this little Republic'. The reason Lucca attracted visitors, as it had attracted Francis Mortoft a hundred years earlier, was because it was known as a model state—'a peaceful, law-abiding, industrious, prosperous and independent little state', as John Fleming observes,

---

[13] *Travels Through France and Italy* (repr. 1949).

'which had successfully governed itself as a republic for several hundred years.'[14] The visitors' firearms were removed at the gate of entry and returned to them at the gate of departure.

Dr Johnson's friend Mrs Thrale, who came to Lucca on a honeymoon tour after her marriage to Gabriel Piozzi, called it 'a fairy commonwealth'. One was struck, she said, by the gold lettering about the main gate—*Libertas*. The streets were paved and kept clean, and one could walk about the city without being pestered by beggars or by thieves at night. No murder had been committed there within living memory, and only one robbery in sixteen years. When a thief was sentenced to be executed, an executioner had to be imported from Florence since no Lucchese citizen could bear to perform this act!

Once one arrived in Italy, there were various ways of getting from place to place. Usually at posting houses a horse could be hired, or three or four or five travellers would hire a coach. Or one could employ a *vetturino*, a sort of travel agent, to arrange the journey, paying a set amount in advance for the hiring of horses and vehicles, as well as accommodation along the way. Sometimes bandits were bribed by the *vetturini* not to attack their coaches. When their carriage arrived at Florence in 1817, fourteen-year-old Harriet Charlotte Beaujolais Campbell, whose mother was lady-in-waiting to the Princess of Wales, wrote in her diary:

> And thus ends my account of this journey without my ever having had to write of a single adventure neither of banditti or robbers. To tell the truth after all the fright I felt in the expectation of them I feel rather provoked.[15]

Eventually much of the rigour and risk was taken out of travel in Italy owing to the coming of the railways. Tuscany was one of the first Italian states to lay down the iron way. Money was raised for the railway between Florence and Leghorn and work started

[14] Cesare Sardi, *Vita Lucchese nel settecento*, Introduction by John Fleming (1968).
[15] *A Journey to Florence in 1817* (repr. 1951).

just thirteen years after the Stockton and Darlington railway, built by George Stephenson, was opened to passengers. Another Stephenson—George's son Robert—was largely responsible for the Tuscan engineering feat.

Robert Stephenson and two of his engineers surveyed the Florence–Leghorn route and the George Stephenson works supplied locomotives which were greatly praised, 'truly admirable for perfect workmanship and the well-arranged solidity,' according to the Company's progress report. 'They are of six [double] wheels . . . for the greatest power.'[16] By 1848 these locomotives were pulling a train once a day from Leghorn to Florence and back, leaving Leghorn at 5.45 a.m.

A difficulty in the course of the line's construction had provided a foretaste of modern times. The rail bridge over the Arno was of advanced design, with five spans covering 96 feet; but two of the iron architraves for the bridge were late in arriving from England, and the ceremonial inauguration of the completed railway, by Grand Duke Leopold II, had to go forward on 14 July 1847 despite a conspicuous gap over the Arno. The account of the ceremony in the Florentine paper of the time, the *Gazzetta di Firenze*, is formal and cursory, but one can imagine the discomfiture of the guests aboard the beautifully polished and beflagged train, obliged to get out when they came to the unfinished bridge, walk across the service bridge, and resume their journey in a second train on the other side. Even so, they must all have been wildly enthusiastic that day. For this was the culmination of a long history of toil and struggle. The old rough roads into Italy, the desolate way into Tuscany over which so many visitors had laboured, were soon to be things of the almost unimaginable past.

[16] Ogliati and Sapi, *Segmenti di Lavoro* (History of Italian Transport) (Milan, 1971).

A Sienese Pope

SIENA is the most medieval-seeming of all the larger cities of Tuscany. Famous throughout the world for the pageantry, and brutality, of its Palio, the fierce bareback horse race run twice every summer in which horses often die, the city itself remains unspoiled despite the annual tourist invasion, and its centre entirely peaceful. Serenely circling its three hills, it is steeped in an air of 'might-have-been': it was so nearly the mightiest city of central Italy.

The greatest of the early European banking cities, having important connections with Britain, Siena was overtaken by Florence. It once defeated its great rival in battle in 1260, at Montaperti, but was unable thereafter to press home its advantage, seemingly out of a failure of will, or perhaps out of too much democracy—an inability to take the necessary ruthless decisions. Or it may have been not having a water supply adequate for the needs of industry, or its lack of an outlet to the sea—whereas Florence, after its conquest of Pisa in 1406, seemed to have everything it needed for trade. Also the city had its share of disasters: in 1348 some 65,000 Sienese died in the Great Plague; and two centuries later, when Siena rebelled against the domination of the Emperor Charles V, the city held out for seven months against the besieging Spanish army, and of a population of 40,000 only 8,000 survived. The Emperor ceded the city to Cosimo II, the first Grand Duke of Tuscany, in 1557 and the Florentines were too shrewd ever to let their fine acquisition regain its former strength.

Much remained, however, when Siena's power and influence were gone—as a series of British visitors, among them Milton and Boswell—were to discover. Fynes Moryson, for example, remarking in 1594 of Tuscany generally that 'a stranger may live more commodiously than in any other part of Italy, because the inhabitants are most courteous', declared:

> at Sienna they admit strangers to converse and dance with the chiefe Gentelewomen of the Citie, and because the language, especially at Sienna, is held the most pure, as also for that victuals are very cheape, and strangers need not stand in fear of being murthered . . .[1]

A fitting background to the civility of its inhabitants are Siena's narrow streets, lined with perfectly preserved palaces, and crowning all, its vast Duomo, the Library of which is a monument to the great fifteenth-century humanist Pope, Pius II. Created at the bidding of Pius II's nephew, a Cardinal who later became Pope Pius III, the Library houses the wonderful frescoes by Pinturicchio (aided or advised in some small measure, it is thought, by the young Raphael) showing the life of Pius II. One of these frescoes, which are notable for the vivacity of their portrayal, depicts a little-known episode in the Anglo-Tuscan connection: the journey Pius II made to Britain more than five centuries ago.

Pius II (1405–64), whose *Commentaries* are among the most famous works of the period, had an intensely curious mind. He was born Aeneas Silvius Piccolomini at Corsignano (later Pienza) outside Siena where his now impoverished family, once leading gentlefolk of Siena, still held some land. His early years were spent among the vineyards, and the beauty of the countryside lingered with him always. At the University of Siena he was deeply influenced by the preaching of Father (later Saint) Bernardino, but rejected the idea of joining the Franciscan order, for he was a vital young man with healthy physical appetites, and was basically something of an opportunist. He worked hard at law, but amused himself with writing, producing more than 2,000 lines of Latin verse, the *Nymphiplexis*, on a Ferrarese friend's affair with his mistress. His most successful work of that

---

[1] *An Itinerary* (1617).

time was *De Duobus Amantibus*, the 'Tale of Two Lovers', whose indelicacy he found it hard in later years to live down.[2]

By the age of twenty-six Aeneas must have found that Siena afforded him too little scope; he seized the chance offer of a post as first secretary to the dissident Bishop of Fermo, Domenico Capranica, whom he was to accompany to the Council of Basel. The first of the Pinturicchio frescoes shows the handsome young secretary riding on a white charger towards the port of embarkation and looking back at Siena. There is a dark cloud in the sky above him, but the blue sky ahead gives promise for the future. Circumstances outside his control forced Aeneas to exchange that first post for another, as secretary to Cardinal Albergati. Though a strict Carthusian, Albergati was a man of charm and high intelligence, generous to young scholars, and for four years Aeneas worked happily with him in Florence, acquiring his first experience of diplomacy. He then accompanied the Cardinal to Milan and with him crossed the St Bernard pass to Basel to attend the Council.

From there they went on to the Congress of Arras, where a peace treaty was being discussed that would bring to an end the Hundred Years War between England and France. In 1435 Aeneas was dispatched to Scotland on a secret mission to persuade King James I to make raids over the border into England, thus creating a diversion that might force the English to make peace with the French. He was at Calais waiting for a ship when the English authorities there placed him under house arrest as a possible spy, but Cardinal Henry Beaufort, passing through the port on his way home from the Council at Basel, where he had met Aeneas, found and rescued the young emissary.

Beaufort procured a permit for Aeneas to go from Dover to London, where he could apply for a safe-conduct to Scotland. In the event this was refused, but Aeneas was able to visit the 'sights' of the English capital, which he enumerated in his *Commentaries* (Book V): 'the noble temple of St Paul's, the marvellous tombs of the Kings [at Westminster] and the river Thames which flows less swiftly than it rises; the bridge that is

---

[2] Manuscripts of many of Pius II's writings are in the State Archives of Siena, in the Palazzo Piccolomini.

like a city.' (The latter must have been London Bridge, with its houses and shops.)

Lacking a safe-conduct overland, Aeneas had no alternative but to re-cross the Channel and find a ship plying directly from one of the Channel ports to Scotland. *En route* to the coast, his insatiable curiosity took him to the village of Strood in Kent where, it was rumoured, men were born with tails. He does not tell us if he found any of these; obviously he was anxious to get on to Canterbury to see 'the golden shrine of St Thomas of Canterbury', which, he thought, surpassed in interest both St Paul's and Westminster, and he was entranced by the jewels which covered the shrine.

He sailed for Scotland eventually from Sluys, in what is now the Netherlands, but within a few days of leaving port his ship was blown off course almost to Norway. For fourteen hours the gale blew unabated and Aeneas feared so greatly for his life that he made a vow to Our Lady that if he reached safety he would walk barefoot to her nearest shrine, to give thanks for his survival. On the twelfth day the ship made harbour at Dunbar. The nearest church dedicated to the Virgin proved to be at Whitekirk, some twelve miles distant over a rough track. It was February and icy cold, with a chill wind blowing in from the North Sea. When Aeneas arrived at Whitekirk he was so weak, and his limbs so stiff with pain, that his servants had to carry him, and he rested in the church for two hours. He was to suffer rheumatic pains all his life from the effects of this pilgrimage.[3]

Arriving at last in Edinburgh, Aeneas was received with due graciousness by James I. Pinturicchio was to idealize the scene in the second of the frescoes in Siena, in which the King is a fine figure listening to the eloquent blond Italian; Aeneas himself afterwards described the King as 'small and fat, hot-tempered and greedy for vengeance'.[4] James's memories of eighteen years'

---

[3] As Pope, he went often for treatment to the spas of Petrolio and Viterbo in central Italy. The famous Dr Giovanni de Ferrariis of Grado, Court Physician to Francesco Sforza of Milan, wrote to him that, 'to be sure, most Holy Father, when I heard about your unfortunate trouble in the sinews or joints of your feet, all my care and all my concern was for getting rid of it, or at least, for improving the condition' (Bodleian MS Digby 135 fo. 1ᵛ). Noting that Aristotle had advocated mineral water and sulphur baths, the great doctor advised the Pope to put his feet frequently in hot water.

[4] *De Viris Illustribus*, No. xxxii.

captivity in England made him well disposed to Aeneas' proposal that he should begin border warfare. According to the *Commentaries* Aeneas was given money to meet the expenses of his stay, and a retinue of fifty nobles, as well as two horses; he was also presented with a pearl which he later gave to his mother. He appears to have enjoyed some feminine companionship in Edinburgh, for a son of his was born after his departure from the city; the boy died when he was eight.

In later years Aeneas described the relatively crude Scottish court where the King lived 'more roughly than the poorer citizens of Nuremberg'. The country itself he found cold, deficient in crops and with few trees, but one must remember that he was there in the heart of winter. 'The commoners are poor and uneducated,' he wrote in the *Commentaries* (Book I).

> They stuff themselves with meat and fish, and look on bread as a delicacy. The men are small of stature and brave, the women white and beautiful and very prone to love. To kiss a woman means less there than to touch her hand in Italy. They have not wine except what is imported. Their horses are all hackneys by breed and small. A few are kept for stud, the rest are gelded, and they are never groomed, whether with iron or wooden combs, nor yet do they have reins. . . . Hides, wool, salt, fish and pearls are exported from Scotland to Flanders.

Aeneas had obviously never seen coal before, which he described:

> Beneath the soil a sulphureous stone is found which they dig out and burn for fuel. The towns lack walls and the houses are built for the most part without lime; the farms are roofed with turfs and in the country an ox-hide serves to close the door. . . . There is nothing the Scots hear more gladly than disparagement of the English.

So we smile. Nothing has changed in this respect five centuries later!

Disguising himself as a merchant to avoid attention south of the border, Aeneas at length started for home. His first night on

English soil, after crossing (apparently) the Solway Firth, was memorable. He was given hospitality by a peasant, and, while at supper with his host and the parish priest, was joined by the villagers who arrived, as they do today in Tuscany, to view the strangers. They brought gifts of hens and geese to be cooked, and Aeneas had red wine and white bread among his own provisions. (Though where the white bread had been baked, and how, it is difficult to know since he says the villagers had never seen such a thing before.) The feasting went on very late and he was tired. Suddenly the men and children rose, saying they were going to a peel tower for safety since the Scots often raided them when the Solway was at low tide. The 'girls and handsome matrons' were left round the fire and Aeneas was left with them. He was reassured about his safety, 'since', as he says, 'they do not count rape as harm'! The interpreter had to translate the local dialect, and finally two girls accompanied the Italian to a chamber strewn with straw which, he recalled, smelled of goat. They were apparently ready to sleep with him, but 'his mind was less on women than on the thieves he expected at any moment', and he drove them away, reluctant and disappointed. A disturbance during the night brought out barking dogs and hissing geese but it proved to be a false alarm. Aeneas had a few hours' rest and set out early for Newcastle, where he felt he was returning to civilization.[5]

At Durham he visited the tomb of the Venerable Bede, and went on to York where the Minster impressed him as 'a chapel full of light whose walls are of glass held up by extremely slender pillars'. There is reason to think that he had York in mind when many years later he referred to the cathedral in his native Corsignano (Pienza), built at his instigation, as 'glass held together by slender columns' (*Commentaries*, Book V). He continued his journey to London in the company of an itinerant judge who spoke scornfully of Aeneas' patron, Cardinal Albergati, little guessing the identity of his young companion. At London he

---

[5] Aeneas' adverse comments on both Scotland and England, which he found uncivilized by Italian standards, are partly explained in a letter some eighteen years later to a Sienese cousin, Goro, who had been at University with him: while in Britain, he was tormented by toothache and lost most of his teeth, 'not without excruciating agony'.

discovered that he needed a royal permit to leave the country, and a bribe was necessary to obtain a passage to Calais.

Not all Aeneas' encounters with the English were unhappy, however. At Frankfort, where he went as representative of the Council of Basel, he made friends with Adam de Moleyns, or Mulin, Bishop of Chichester and Keeper of the Privy Seal, with whom he afterwards corresponded. Moleyns must have been educated at Oxford where the little band of humanists found a generous patron in Humphrey, Duke of Gloucester. Aeneas wrote to Moleyns:

> I read your letter with eagerness, and wondered that the Latin style had penetrated even into Britain. It is true that there have been amongst the English some who have cultivated the eloquence of Cicero, amongst whom common consent would place the Venerable Bede. . . . For this advance all gratitude is due to the illustrious Duke of Gloucester, who zealously received polite learning into your kingdom. I hear that he cultivates poets and venerates orators; hence many Englishmen now turn out really eloquent. For, as are the princes, so are the people; and servants progress through imitating their masters. . . . Great is eloquence; nothing so much rules the world. Political action is the result of persuasion; his opinion prevails with the people who best knows how to persuade them.[6]

It was somewhat ironic that as Keeper of the Privy Seal, Moleyns must have signed Gloucester's death warrant in 1447, though he had not conspired against him. And, as Aeneas tells us in *De Europa* (1458), the head of Moleyns who had helped negotiate the marriage of the Lancastrian King Henry VI to Margaret of Anjou, was one of the first to fall when the Yorkist Edward IV took over the throne.

Meanwhile, Aeneas pursued his own diplomatic and literary career. At Frankfort he was made Poet Laureate by the Emperor, who declaimed (in a scene also painted by Pinturicchio in the frescoes at Siena): 'We with our own hands decorate Aeneas

---

[6] *Opera. Epist.* LXIV; cited by Mandell Creighton, 'The Early Renaissance in England,' *Historical Lectures and Addresses* (1904).

with the evergreen leaves of the laurel so that his name and honour may flourish for ever, and that his brilliant example may encourage others of like talent.'[7]

Having taken holy orders in 1446, at the age of forty-one, Aeneas was rewarded with a bishopric for his part in reconciling the Emperor Frederick III with the Pope. Eventually he organized the Emperor's coronation journey, and in his cathedral at Siena (as the frescoes show) he married the Emperor to the attractive and vivacious sixteen-year-old Leonora of Portugal. Frederick had gone to the coast at Talamone to await his bride's arrival, but after sixty days of battling storms at sea, her ship had to land at Livorno instead. Aeneas hurried to Pisa to greet the Princess, who met the Emperor at last at Siena, 'in a spacious open plain' on the north side of the city.

In 1456 Aeneas was created Cardinal. When, two years later, he was elected Pope there were great rejoicings throughout the country, especially among the humanist scholars from Britain. John Free wrote that Pius II, as Aeneas was to be known, was the most worthy of all men living to occupy St Peter's throne; and, before leaving Italy in 1460, John Tiptoft, Earl of Worcester, delivered a Latin oration so moving that the Pope was in tears. But the hopes of the humanists were not to be realized during Pius' period as Pope.

Lawyer, orator, poet, a man of many parts, full-blooded and enjoying the good life, though abstemious in his personal habits, the new Pope had grown in spirituality over the years. His great joy, in the six years he was to have in the Papacy, was the creation of the town of Pienza and its bishopric on the site of the poor village of his birth, Corsignano. He took personal charge of the building of Pienza and made immensely practical suggestions to his architect, Bernardo of Florence.[8]

In the Cathedral Museum at Pienza is a superb cope, made in England in the fourteenth century, which was a gift to Pius from Tommaso Paleologo, one-time ruler of the Morea. After

---

[7] Regesta Chronologico-Diplomatica Frederici III.
[8] Generally believed to have been Bernardo Rosellino, one of the great architects of the Renaissance.

the fall of Constantinople the Emperor's brothers took control of the Morea, and afterwards Tommaso, fleeing from the Turks, came with his family to Rome as poor refugees. The Pope was exceedingly generous to them and in gratitude Tommaso offered Pius the treasures he had brought from the Morea; among them was this exquisitely embroidered cope, which Pius himself described:

> This sacred vestment surely seems to excel all others in Christendom in its work and craftsmanship. The closely woven gold texture is resplendent with small figures of saints so true to nature that one might think them alive; further, it has been made so elaborate in art and work that the whole composition, woven and embellished with countless pearls, draws the admiration of us all, and it cannot be valued at a small price; it would be judged incomparable were it stretched out at full length.

In the thirteenth and fourteenth centuries English embroidery was the finest in the western world, and examples were found in the possession of the greatest rulers and Church potentates. An inventory of embroidery taken in the Vatican in 1295 included more works of *opus anglicanum*, as it was called, than of any other. The cope given to Pius II was so large, being 11 feet 6 inches wide, 5 feet 4½ inches long, and 15 feet 6 inches in circumference, that the Pope, who was short in stature, may have found it impossible to wear; so he donated it to the new Cathedral.

It is indeed a wonderful piece of work, containing within its circumference 47 subjects dramatically worked in architectural frameworks, and 'a profusion of naturalistic birds and animals, foliage of oak, ivy and vine, heraldic lions' masks, rosettes, and six-winged seraphs'.[9] Among the subjects are the life of the Virgin, shown in the most intricate detail (the scene of her crowning is particularly enchanting), the childhood of Christ, and the lives of St Catherine and St Margaret. The needlework in gold, silver and varied silks is on a twofold linen foundation, and the pearls that were originally attached were very numerous. In 1884 many of these remained, but in that year the cope was

[9] Mrs A. H. Christie, *English Mediaeval Embroidery*, No. 95 (1938).

stolen from the Museum and stripped of every pearl before it was found in Florence four days later. However, the needlework was, and remains, in good condition, and many visitors to Florence still go to Pienza expressly to see it.

Another action of Pius II, in his brief tenure as Pope, was to set in motion in 1459 the necessary procedures for the canonization of Catherine of Siena. Born in 1347, she was a nun of a cloistered order who, in response to a vision, had come out into the world to seek some antidote to the moral corruption she saw as affecting the religious orders. For a time she played a prominent part in the politics of the Vatican. She was credited with bringing back Pope Gregory XI from Avignon to Rome, though she was disillusioned by his use of force and shocked by the massacre of civilians at Cesena carried out by Gregory's hired army under the command of the English mercenary, Sir John Hawkwood. After Gregory's death a great schism began in the papacy, with the Medici Pope, Clement VII, establishing himself and his Curia at Avignon while his rival, Gregory's original successor, Urban VI, clung to power in Rome. Catherine used her not inconsiderable influence upon Urban to persuade him to summon to Rome prelates and monks of integrity.

In these efforts there was an English connection, for one of the monks she recommended to the Pope was an Englishman from Cambridge, William of Flete, an Augustan friar at the convent of San Salvatore at Lecceto, a few miles west of Siena, who became her disciple. William's life was more austere than the rules of his eremitical Order required; he occupied his time in penance and study in a cave in the woods, only returning to the convent in the evening to attend the religious offices. In one of her letters to him, Catherine argued that he attached too much importance to mortification of the flesh, and urged him not to allow love of solitude to draw him and his fellow hermits from duties of obedience and charity.

Though fiercely loyal to Catherine, William refused to go to Rome. He declared the papal summons was a device of the Devil to deprive the servants of God of their spiritual consolations. Catherine was too hurt to write to him direct, but she forgave him. When she died in the Vatican in 1380 at the age of thirty-three, she was buried in the Roman church of Santa Maria sopra Minerva; but Siena held its own funeral services for her and William of Flete went there to preach the oration, preserved today in the Archives at Siena. Some sources say that William returned to England after having introduced stricter reforms at Lecceto; others that he died at Lecceto. One of his manuscripts preserved in the University Library at Cambridge proclaims the calamities coming to England, including the loss of the Catholic faith.

Having refused the Pope's summons to Rome, the saintly William could not have been canonized. With Catherine of Siena there was no such difficulty, and under Pius II her canonization duly took place in 1461. But the great spiritual mission of Pius' reign, his attempt that same year of 1461 to rally the whole of Christendom, including England, in a major crusade to defeat the Turks, was not a success. He was let down on all sides and even the Venetian ships were late in arriving at Ancona, the port of embarkation. The final Pinturicchio fresco shows him waiting for the ships; by the time they came there were not enough crusaders to fill them. Three days later, at the age of fifty-nine, Pius died, in agony from 'the stone'.

A memorial was erected to Pope Pius and his abortive crusade, but was destroyed during the Second World War. His *Commentaries*, which he wrote as relaxation, are his greatest memorial; together with the *Letter to Mahomet*, a clear statement of the Christian as opposed to the Muslim point of view composed in 1460 and circulated throughout Europe, they are impressive evidence of his faith in the power of the written word. And, for the visitor to Siena, this gifted, curious man will always come vividly to life in the frescoes in the Library of the Duomo.

The Merchant
Bankers

I F British life was enriched culturally and aesthetically, from the early Middle Ages onward, by the Tuscan connection, it was also enriched literally—to get down to brass tacks—by Tuscan money and knowledge of money. Whatever we owe to our early access to Italian libraries of humanism and to their new perspectives on art, there is strong reason for putting banking first and arguing that the Renaissance in England would not have come about had we not learnt an earlier lesson from the Italians: the value of investing an honest florin.

There had been business relations of a sort for many years between Tuscany and England. As early as 1190 Richard I was borrowing from 'Lombard' merchants in Italy on his way to the Great Crusade,[1] and his son John also negotiated with the *Mercatores Tuscie*, papal tax collectors and lenders of money. These merchants were also deeply involved in the trade in English wool, especially that of high quality produced by the monks, which had long been bought by Italians at the great fairs of Champagne and the Low Countries to supply the weavers of Florence.

Usury being a sin in the eyes of the Church, and usurers liable to the charge of being heretics, no interest was charged on the loans made by the 'Lombards';[2] they were merely transactions covered by 'bills of exchange'. Despite the circumlocution, a royal edict was issued in 1240 expelling foreign merchants on

---

[1] Pipe Rolls 3 & 4, R. 1, p. 145.
[2] A somewhat pejorative term loosely applied by the insular British to Italians who came, in fact, from the republics of Genoa, Lucca, Florence, Siena and Venice. The street in London in which they settled has been known ever since as Lombard Street.

the grounds of usury; but the measure was difficult to enforce since both King Henry III and the religious communities were still paying off their debts to the 'Lombards'. Eleven years later, indeed, Tuscan merchants were to be found in the best houses in London, living under papal protection. The Salimbeni family of Siena was particularly successful at this time, and when they returned to their native city used their gains, ill-gotten or not, in acquiring neighbouring castles and estates. The Sienese merchants indeed survived their excommunication by the Pope in 1262 through the customary use of bribery, only to be banished from England later by Henry under pressure from their rivals the Florentines.

The various Tuscan usurers or bankers who found their way to London in the thirteenth century almost invariably dealt directly with the monarch, and often became his indispensable confidants. In return for their readiness to raise funds for the crown, they were found sinecures such as control of the Mint. When Edward I initiated export duties on wool and leather and hides, the collectors of these taxes at London and thirteen other ports were supervised by one Luke, or Luca, of Lucca (his family name isn't recorded). This Luca became a close adviser to King Edward, and on his death in 1279[3] was succeeded by Orlandino di Podio of the Riccardi company of Lucca. The diplomatic skills and experience of such men made them useful as emissaries abroad, and Tuscans were given royal letters recommending them to the Pope and the King of France. One distinguished Master of the Mint, Walter de' Bardi,[4] continued in this office under Richard II whom he also served in a diplomatic capacity. In 1366 he had been granted denization (a form of naturalization) by Edward III.

The Tuscan merchant bankers were now authorised by the King to hold private exchanges[5] (the Florentines continued, for example, to trade in wool). When the King demanded a loan, to finance some warlike foray into Scotland or participation in the Crusades against Islam, the Italians would raise the cash from deposits in various places in northern Europe. To do this they

---

[3] Cal. Close Rolls (CCR), 1272–81, pp. 532–44.
[4] Cal. Patent Rolls (CPR), 1374–77, p. 312.
[5] CCR 1374–77.

had to refer back to their superiors in Lucca, Florence, or Siena; and some of them were connected with the Papal Curia, by whom quite often a slice of the proceeds could be authorised. In 1277, in fact, some of the proceeds of the papal tenths were in the hands of seven Tuscan companies, or 'societies' as they were called in the English records: the Riccardi of Lucca, the Pucci and Lambertini of Florence, the Mozzi and Scala also of Florence, the Ammanati of Pistoia and the Bonsignori of Siena; there were also the Scoti of Piacenza. These companies had deposited 9,200 marks in the treasury of the New Temple in London, in 77 large sacks, one small sack and a leather purse.[6] This apparently became a regular arrangement, and when Edward I announced his intention of departing on a Crusade to the Holy Land, Pope Nicholas IV issued an order to his bankers in England, then the Riccardi of Lucca, authorising them to pay the King on 24 June 1289 the first half of the 'crusading tenth' collected in the British Isles.[7]

For seventy-five years, from the first quarter of the thirteenth century, Siena was the pioneer and the chief banking centre in Europe, and when the largest of its companies, the Bonsignori of the *gran tavola* (the *banca* or bank was a 'great table' over which the business was conducted), failed in 1298, the city never fully recovered.[8] Two and a half centuries later, Siena was besieged and taken by the Spanish, and then ceded to Florence, Cosimo II having aided the Spanish. In an attempt to bolster the economy of the city Cosimo backed the bank which had been founded in 1472, the Monte dei Paschi di Siena, and personally guaranteed the loans it made to sheep farmers (hence the name *paschi* or, as it was, *pascoli*, meaning pastures). By 1620, the Monte dei Paschi, the first modern-style bank in the world, was using printed cheques and paying interest on deposits. But Cosimo had astutely limited it in its statute to dealing only with the citizens of Siena, to make sure that it would not compete with

---

[6] W. E. Lunt, *Financial Relations of the Papacy with England to 1327* (1926).

[7] King's Remembrancer's Customs Accounts, Mint 208/6, Public Record Office.

[8] Raymond de Roover, *The Rise and Fall of the Medici Bank* (1966).

Florence in international financial activities, and this limitation remained in force until 1840.

The great heyday of Florentine banking was in the fourteenth century, under the Medici. In 1338 eighty money-changing banks were active in Florence, and membership in their guild, the Arte del Cambio, was compulsory. But the first Medici bank was in Rome. Giovanni di Bicci de' Medici, from one branch of that family (and the one who was the real founder of the great dynasty), having gone to Rome to learn the business, then transferred it to the Mercato Nuovo in his home town. The bank lasted for almost a century, until 1494, by which time Lorenzo the Magnificent was concerned with other things than money. One could say that the wealth of the Medici bank (and other Florentine banks) was dissipated in the glorious explosion of the Renaissance; as when, for example, in 1442 a branch of the Medici bank in Pisa gave an advance to the sculptor Donatello for the purchase of Carrara marble.

The branch of the Medici bank in London was opened in 1446, in the reign of Henry VI, though business had been done in the City by the 'correspondent' in Bruges for many years. The London bank started with a capital of £2,500 sterling, of which the Medici supplied £2,166 13s 4d, and the manager (appointed from Lombard Street), Gerozzo di Jacopo de' Pigli, the remaining £333 6s 8d—a small enough sum considering that he took a fifth of the profits. A quite elaborate four-year contract was drawn up for Pigli's engagement. If he had not produced his small share of the capital by a certain date, 12 per cent interest was to be charged. He was to have a residence in London, but could go to Southampton on business or ride into the Cotswolds to buy wool without informing Florence. He was given detailed advice as to whom he could lend money to: only to merchants or craftsmen of good repute, and on no account to any *signori* (nobles). Every year on 24 March the books had to be balanced and a copy of the balance sheet sent to headquarters in Florence. The manager was also expected to invest the profits of his branch in buying wool for Florence, no doubt at a further substantial profit. Wool galleys were introduced in that century, so that the bulk of the wool no longer went overland; and though export duties still applied to it, Tuscans like Pigli in London were given permits to export freely in return for their services to the King.

The Wars of the Roses brought an end to these happy commercial days, and as York replaced Lancaster the new King disclaimed all responsibility for the debts of his predecessor. By 1457, according to the tax declaration of Gerozzo de' Pigli, the entire capital of the Medici bank had been lost. But the Medici must have replaced this capital, because in 1462 Gherardo Canigiani, described as 'factor and attorney of the fellowship of the Medici of Florence', was lending 20 pounds and again 100 marks to Edward IV in the first months of his reign, no doubt to pay his troops and perhaps his tailor. Not long afterwards a gift of 200 pounds 'for divers secret matters' was paid to James Kennedy, Bishop of St Andrews, by the hand of this same Canigiani,[9] who was apparently privy to the King's designs.

The King's subsequent demands for money were not refused. In return for a loan of 800 marks Edward granted the Medici company the right to ship 200 sacks of wool from Sandwich to the Staple of Calais and 'beyond the mountains' (i.e. to Italy) without paying customs.[10] Canigiani also exported cloth and lead, and was at the same time importing from Italy olives, prunes, oil, saltpetre, brimstone and the rich fabrics and silks so much admired by Edward and his nobles. In 1464 he brought into Sandwich '21½ virgates of velvet in grain and 27 virgates of crimson velvet'.[11] As the King was so fond of extravagant and beautiful clothes and jewels (and of women to match), it was enterprising of him to go into partnership with Canigiani in certain export and import activities.

Before the end of 1464, Canigiani became a householder in London; he and John de' Bardi were the only Florentines in the city to pay the tax of 40 shillings levied each year. He had also become independent of the Medici, who had abandoned a great many of their lesser activities. In Florence Cosimo's son Piero (Piero the Gouty) left the banking business to a certain Francesco Sassetti, and Piero's son, Lorenzo (the Magnificent), leant even more upon Sassetti, who built up a great personal fortune and

9 CPR I, 348–9.
10 Writs of Privy Seal, file 797. 1400.
11 Customs Accounts, Sandwich, 128/6 128/10 128/12.

was another of the patrons of the Renaissance. It was Lorenzo's indifference, however, which brought the bank to its ultimate decline. The final blow came from London, where, Canigiani having got out smartly in 1472, the Bruges manager, Tommaso Portinari, misguidedly agreed to take over the assets and liabilities of the London office, including the claims on Edward IV. Losses of 51,533 florins had to be written off when the wars flared up again and Henry of Lancaster briefly regained the throne. Though Edward IV won back his crown at the battle of Tewkesbury, as far as the Medici were concerned the damage was done, and thereafter their activities in London were confined to the buying and shipping of wool to Pisa in the galleys.

The reinstated Edward continued to lean heavily on Canigiani, who apparently had other resources besides the Medici, for two months after Tewkesbury £6,600 was found for the King, and then the royal jewels were redeemed from pawn at a cost of £4,500.[12] Sometime before Easter of 1474, Canigiani married a well-off Englishwoman, Dame Elizabeth Stokton,[13] presumably a widow, and the King sent him a wedding gift of jewels which cost £73 12s, as well as, two years later, a cup of silver gilt for the baptism of his first child. Letters of denization (naturalization) were granted to Canigiani and his heirs. The King, accepting a sum of £360, had also granted him the manor of Great Lynford, Buckinghamshire, and the advowson of right of presentation to the parish church.

Canigiani eventually joined the Mercers' Guild and henceforward was described as 'merchant, citizen and mercer of London, sometime of the fellowship of the Medici of Florence, and factor and attorney of the same'.[14] In spite of some unpleasantness with Portinari, who resented the favours he received from the King and also thought that he should pay some of the £2,000 still owed to the Medici, Canigiani appeared to enjoy a good life. He outlived the King his friend, who had issued a five-year protection for him, his servants and property against attack by the members of the Medici bank, and died a natural death in good season. His merchant banking business and his

---

[12] Warrants for issues, 13 Edw IV 28 Feb.
[13] CPR 11 466.
[14] C. L. Schofield, *Life of Edward IV* (1923).

manor passed into other hands and the Canigiani name faded into decent obscurity.

The 'Lombards' had done their bit. The business of financing imports and exports as well as kings and clerics which Canigiani and his predecessors had developed in England had become a part of the pattern of the expanding life of the island. The part that permitted the expansion, in fact.

·☾ IV ☽·

Pretenders
Old and Young

Charles shall yet reign, and Justice weep no more . . .
Reviving Britain shall no longer fear
To lose her ancient race.

(lines written 'Upon the marriage of the King with the Princess Louisa of Stolberg Guidern, by a gentleman in foreign parts. October 20, 1772').

IN Florence, at the corner of Via Gino Capponi and Via Antonio Micheli, is an imposing house with a large garden, known as the Palazzo San Clemente. In the entrance hall of the palazzo, now the Faculty of Architecture of the University of Florence, high up above the manifestos and spray-gunned Communist slogans, is a great fresco of the royal arms of England. *Dieu et mon Droit*, it reads, and below: *Carolus III Nat. 1720 Mag Brittanniae et Hib. et Rex Fid. Defen* and *Honi Soit qui Mal y Pense*. Carolus III is, of course, Charles Edward Stuart, the Young Pretender, the Bonnie Prince Charlie of romance, who lived in Florence much of the time from 1775 until his death—still claiming he was the rightful King of England—in 1788. The house, the former Palazzo Guadagni, was the only one on the continent of Europe actually owned by the Stuarts during their exile.

The royal house of Stuart has been a subject for both tragedy and high romance. Two of the line were executed: Mary Queen of Scots at Fotheringay, and, more publicly, her grandson Charles I outside his palace of Whitehall. The restoration to the throne of Charles's son, the able but philandering Charles II, was followed by the undignified flight of his brother and successor, James II, into self-imposed exile on the Continent; there James II's son, James Edward Stuart, known to history as the Old Pretender, and his two sons, Charles and Henry, were brought up. The influence on the Stuarts of their long stay in Italy, where

33

both Prince Charles and his brother Henry were born and died, was more profound than may generally have been realized.

The influence was natural, for James Edward Stuart's mother was Italian. The saintly and beautiful Mary of Modena came to England in 1673, a trembling, unwilling fifteen-year-old, to marry Charles II's brother James, Duke of York, a widower of forty. It was an important match, for Charles's Queen was childless, and James was heir to the throne; his first wife, Anne Hyde, had borne him only two daughters. The King himself greeted Mary at Greenwich and thought his brother a lucky man. She in her turn admitted later, in exile, to having found the King most attractive; she was doubtless reassured by his easy manner and lost some of her fears.

Her marriage to James became a loving one despite their disparity in age. Many years afterwards she told the nuns at Chaillot that she had become 'very fond of my husband and my affection for him increased with every year that we lived together'.[1] James was able and hard-working, but he lacked his wife's sense of humour and grace. Both were devout Catholics. Mary knew that her duty was to produce an heir to the throne. During the eleven years of her marriage she suffered the loss of a son and three daughters in infancy, as well as three miscarriages. At last, in June 1688, three years after her husband succeeded Charles II, she gave birth to a healthy son, christened James Francis Edward. The Dowager Queen Catherine of Braganza was godmother and the Pope godfather to the child.

James Edward's infancy was difficult: it was believed that milk had caused convulsions in the Queen's earlier children, so this baby was given only water-gruel, barley and oatmeal, sugar, currants and Canary wine. At one time there were thirty medicine bottles on his nursery table. Eventually he was sent upriver to Richmond Palace in order to have purer air. There, however, he soon became dangerously ill; as the Queen wrote later, 'I asked the physicians if they yet had hopes of doing anything for him. They all told us they reckoned him as dead. I sent to the village for a wetnurse . . . He took her milk: it revived him and happily she reared him.'[2]

---

[1] Chaillot Papers, vol. II, p. 369.
[2] ibid.

Mary thereafter refused to be separated from her son. But James meanwhile had carried his Catholic policies too far, and the Protestants rebelled. In 1689 William of Orange, husband of James's daughter by his first marriage, Mary, landed at Torbay with an army which James decided he could not oppose; he sent his wife and son to safety in France, and he himself followed.

Louis XIV welcomed the presence in France of a Catholic Pretender whom he could use as a thorn in the flesh of the new Protestant regime in Britain. He gave James a palace at St-Germain-en-Laye, outside Paris, where the exiled ruler's court could gather round him, and granted him an annual pension of 600,000 livres. James of course expected eventually to be recalled to the throne as his brother had been after Cromwell's death; but when he died in 1701 the House of Orange was still in power. In 1702 James's unmarried second daughter, Anne, succeeded to the throne, and reigned until her death in 1714.

If James Edward Stuart, who came of age in 1706, had been more decisive, if he had not relied so greatly on the promises of the French and the advice of his own divided court, he might have headed a Jacobite uprising that would have forced Queen Anne to declare him her successor. But the young man was often ailing and seemed to lack the necessary will to take power, though in 1708–9 he served with distinction in the French army which the British defeated at Oudenaarde and Malplaquet, earning in the latter engagement his title of 'Chevalier de St Georges'.

There were in all four attempts to reinstate James as King of England, the most important being the 1715 rebellion which followed Queen Anne's death. Under the Protestant Act of Succession the throne then went to the Hanoverian George I, who was unpopular, as he neither spoke English nor appeared to be responsive to English ideas. But James failed to seize his chance. He did not arrive on British soil until December 1715, four months after the Earl of Mar had proclaimed him King and raised his standard at Braemar. The English army made short work of the suicidally ill-organized Scots force, and the rebellion was suppressed in less than a month after James's arrival. He escaped to the Continent from Montrose.

After the death in 1715 of Louis XIV the French wanted to make peace with England, and James was forced to move on. He took refuge for a time in the papal territory of Avignon, and then went on by way of Modena and Rome to Urbino. There he lived—courtesy of the Pope, who also allowed him a pension of 12,000 scudi a year—in the palace built by the Dukes of Montefeltro; a small unfurnished chamber called the King of England's Room can be seen in the palace today.

It was now thought time that James Edward should marry and have an heir. One of his Irish followers, Charles Wogan, was sent to find a suitable Catholic bride, and his choice fell on the lovely sixteen-year-old Maria Clementina Sobieska, granddaughter of John III Sobieski, King of Poland and Lithuania, who had saved Europe from the Turks. As the young princess travelled to Italy, she was stopped at Innsbruck and placed under restraint by the Holy Roman Emperor, at the request of the irate George I of England. But with the gallant Wogan's help she contrived to escape and to reach her bridegroom, whom she married in the cathedral of Montefiascone in September 1719.

Pope Clement XI acknowledged the couple under their titles as King James III and Queen Clementina, and gave them a guard of troops; they settled down in Rome in the house they were also given, the Palazzo Muti in the Piazza dei Santi Apostoli. Both Clementina and her husband enjoyed music, and Rome had at that time the best musicians. There were weekly fêtes and festivals, and the youth and good looks of the royal couple were much admired as they drove about the city. The Pope had also given them a country house where they spent much time, the Palazzo Savelli at Albano, situated in the hills about eighteen miles from Rome, with large airy rooms commanding fine views.

Clementina had her difficulties as a pretender Queen: her English was still not fluent, and she was surrounded by Jacobite courtiers with Scottish or Irish accents. Inevitably she was homesick, since James was closeted with his secretary for hours every day, dealing with correspondence from all parts of Europe. Moreover there were spies everywhere, among them the Prussian expatriate Baron Philip Stosch, alias John Walton, chief agent in Rome for the British Government, by whom the most trivial details of the royal pair's personal life were reported back to England.

Six months after her marriage Clementina found herself pregnant. James's enemies had reported that his wife was too delicate to carry the child successfully, and to forestall the sort of malicious rumours that had circulated about his own birth, James invited a number of Cardinals, royal highnesses and ambassadors to be present when the child, a fine healthy boy, was delivered on 31 December 1720. He was named Charles Edward Louis John Casimir Silvester Maria. The Pope himself paid a visit to give the child his blessing, and the following day cannon were fired from Castel Sant' Angelo as the Romans shouted 'Viva'. Displays of fireworks and fountains running with wine accompanied the New Year celebrations, and thanksgiving medals in silver and bronze were struck, with busts of the child's parents on one side and on the other a mother and child with the words *Spes Brittanniae*, the 'hope of Britain'. Congratulations poured in from all over Europe, while in England the rage of George I at the news of a Stuart heir was only partially mitigated by the false rumour, spread by the spy Walton, that the child was deformed.

James Edward, wishing his son to be educated in English in his formative years, put him in the charge of a Miss Sheldon, from an exiled family living in France at St-Germain-en-Laye whom he had known and trusted all his life. She was to give him daily reports of his son's progress if he was not at home to see him personally. But Miss Sheldon was able apparently to circumvent some of the father's more extreme notions of child-rearing —one of them being that the Prince should be given stimulants at the age of twenty months when he seemed slow in walking.

The violent energy of the young Prince made his fragile mother suffer from headaches. Clementina, still in her teens, was unhappy and unfulfilled as the wife and Queen of a man almost twice her age. Yet she loved James Edward, and in 1722 from Bagni di Lucca sent him a dog with a fervent note apologizing for her 'naughty temper' and vowing: 'I should envy the happiness this dog will have of being near all I hold most dear in the world . . . you know very well that I love you beyond all expression.' The note and the gift so delighted her husband that he hurried to join her, in August of that year, at the Baths of Lucca.

*   *   *

Clementina had wished to visit the famous Baths, the Bagni di Corsena, some 27 kilometres from Lucca, for treatment. She travelled incognito from Rome with only two maids, a valet de chambre, a secretary, a cook and one or two footmen. Stopping on the way at Montefiascone, Siena and Pisa, she arrived in Lucca on Sunday, 22 July, and spent the night at the Osteria della Campana as the Countess of Cornovaglia (Cornwall). The Lucchese Ambassador to Florence, Carlo Orsucci, had reported the coming of the 'Queen of England' to the authorities at Lucca only the day before. Count Cesare Santini welcomed her in the name of the Lucchese government and offered her the services of ladies of Lucca willing to attend her. Clementina preferred, however, to continue the journey informally, and went on the next day to Bagni di Lucca, where she stayed at the Palazzo Buonvisi.

This house, built in the sixteenth century, had belonged to a wealthy and cultured family of Lucca, one of whose members, Antonio Buonvisi, had been the friend of Sir Thomas More. It had been used by other distinguished visitors to the Baths, including the Grand Duchess of Tuscany, Vittoria della Rovere, wife of Ferdinand II, who arrived there in 1669 accompanied by her son and a retinue of 260, among them Francesco Redi, the scientist, philosopher and poet. The Casa Buonvisi, as it is now, was used in wartime as a hospital, and later by the Commune as a school. Hardboard partitions put up to form classrooms have transformed its interior, and it is not easy to envisage the spacious entrance hall with rooms on either side which must have greeted Clementina, and the fountain in an alcove where Redi performed some of his experiments.

When James Edward arrived to join his wife, the Marchese Rafaello di Carlo Mansi presented the greetings of the Republic. The formalities of court life then began, with lavish hospitality being extended to the many foreigners and their attendants accompanying the King, and the allowance made him by the Pope for the visit to the Baths was soon exceeded. Word that Clementina had expressed a wish for a litter from Florence no sooner got about than one made in Lucca was put at her disposal, for the Lucchese were far too proud to have anything brought in from another state: Lucca would provide anything the King and Queen desired. The Marchese Mansi wrote that the royal couple asked about fishing in the Lima, and immediately six deputies had been appointed to organize this.

A letter of instructions to Senator Spada about the conduct of affairs of the court underlines the care which was taken by the authorities over the royal visit:

> If there should arise dissatisfaction between those of the Court of His Majesty and the subjects of the Republic, or strangers, you will interpose your authority and proceed to settle such differences to the entire satisfaction of the Court of His Majesty. . . . It will also be your care that there shall be prepared in the churches and in other places the fald-stool with carpet and cushion, and chair for His Majesty unless he makes protest to the contrary. . . .[3]

James was so impressed by the hospitality of Lucca that he announced that every Thursday during his visit he would hold at the Palazzo Buonvisi the ceremony of 'touching for the King's evil' (scrofula). He had apparently performed the ceremony with some success in the hospitals of Paris in 1715 and 1716, but the proceedings had been nothing to the ceremonial which accompanied it at Bagni di Lucca. The interior of the Palazzo was decorated with rich hangings from the silk looms of Lucca, and a throne draped with crimson silk stood before the niche of the fountain. The ladies of the court were elegantly dressed and wearing high-heeled slippers, the men in powdered periwigs, velvet or satin breeches, silk stockings and buckled shoes. The King was in mulberry-coloured velvet, with a white satin silver-embroidered waistcoat, white satin breeches, silk stockings and diamond-buckled shoes, with fine Mechlin lace at his throat and wrist.

After James was conducted to the throne, and had knelt to pray, the procession of afflicted children approached from the little chapel at Corsena. The King placed his long slender hand on the cheek of each child and hung the 'touch-piece' on its white ribbon round his neck. The Comptroller of the Household then held out a silver ewer and basin so that the King could

---

[3] Archivio di Stato di Lucca. Uffizio Sopra le Differenze dei Confini. No. 107 p. 369 seg.

wash his hands, before he slowly retired. The effect produced on those present was profound: as the High Chancellor, Orazio Donati, said afterwards: 'The King breathed holiness, so filled was he with its spirit and sweetness as he administered it.'[4]

Clementina had intended to take the full course of treatments at the Baths, but before the prescribed number of forty could be taken the weather turned too cold for further immersion. In mid-September it was time for them to depart. James and his wife were entertained in Lucca at the sumptuous Palazzo Mansi (now a museum and art gallery), and at various Lucchese villas. Last of all, they made a solemn religious visit to the most revered shrine in those parts, that of the Volto Santo in the Cathedral of San Martino at Lucca. Then James's envoy, General Forster of Northumberland, took his sovereign's formal thanks to the Republic of Lucca, and in return Senator Spada and Marchese Rafaello Mansi brought to the royal couple the compliments of the government and their wishes for a good journey.

There was an aftermath of the visit, when murmurs of the homage Lucca had paid to the 'Pretender' and 'Madame the Princess', as they were officially called in England, drifted into Britain, and when a manifesto originating in Lucca appeared in support of James's right to rule over the English nation. The British Government showed its anger and disapproval by threatening to prohibit imports of oil and cloth from Lucca, and to reopen its trade with France instead. But John Molesworth, the British envoy at Turin, was able to calm the situation, and on 9 December 1722 addressed a model letter of diplomacy to his fellow diplomat 'Monsieur, l'Ambassadeur de Lucques':

> . . . I receive, Monsieur, with much pleasure the order to signify that though His Majesty [George I] has had much information subject to evil interpretation with regard to the affairs in question, and amongst others that the Declaration of the Pretender scattered in England had been printed at Lucca, His Majesty nevertheless liked to think that the Republic had no share in it, not wishing to attribute to such a wisely governed state the errors of evil-intentioned private people.
>
> Wherefore, Monsieur, you will have the satisfaction of making

4 ibid., Filza No. 458.

known to your principals, that the King, my Master, receives their excuses for the past, and believes that as he has never shown anything but esteem for the honoured Republic, those who govern it will in the future prevent those accidents which could give just occasion for complaint.[5]

The oil and cloth of Lucca seem to have been of some importance to England.

Alas, the healing waters of Bagni di Lucca did not altogether banish the differences between James Edward and Clementina, which came to a crisis when James dismissed Miss Sheldon (who may indeed have been supplying fuel for Clementina's grievances) after the birth of their second son, Henry Benedict Maria Clement Thomas Francis Xavier, in March 1725. Trying to satisfy his followers in Britain as well as those in Europe, James appointed a Protestant in her place, which greatly upset the Catholic Queen. Clementina felt excluded from her husband's confidences, which were constantly given not only to his secretary, John Hay, but also to Hay's wife. Jealous and depressed, the Queen packed a bag and left the Palazzo Muti to retire to the convent of Santa Cecilia in Trastevere. Having pleaded unavailingly for her to return, James himself retired to Bologna with his sons.

In the end a reconciliation was effected when James dismissed the Protestant James Murray, Mrs Hay's brother, whom he had appointed as Charles's tutor, and sent the Hays away. But by the time Clementina left the convent to join him, James had already departed for Scotland to try to organize a rising at the death of George I in June 1727. It was January 1728 before he returned, unsuccessful, to Italy. Husband and wife were then reunited, after two years, and Clementina at that point submitted to James's wishes regarding her sons' education. Turning to a life of piety and good works, she inflicted on her once-gay spirit and delicate constitution a too-severe mortification. She became a thin grave lady, suffering from malnutrition, and died in January 1735 when she was only thirty-four.

[5] ibid., Filza 382.

When James received word of her death, Murray wrote, 'I thought he would have fainted . . . The princes are almost sick with weeping and want of sleep and on all sides there is nothing but lamentation.'[6] The Pope ordered a state funeral, and Clementina was buried in St Peter's, though her heart was removed and placed in a green marble urn in the Church of the Santi Apostoli, near the Palazzo Muti where the spirited Polish princess had lived, in joy and sorrow, for sixteen years.

After her death the melancholy, hypochondriacal James sank into introspective gloom and had no heart for political affairs. Jacobite hopes now turned on Clementina's son, Prince Charles, fifteen at the time of his mother's death. The boy's education had been carried on according to his father's ideas. Latin he could not and would not master, but French and Italian he spoke fluently, and English with an Irish-Scottish accent, and he had learned to read and write well in these languages. (James, never forgetful of the hope of putting Charles on the throne of Britain, always spoke and wrote to his sons in English, and ordered English food such as roast beef, considered a luxury in Rome.) By the age of nine Charles was able to play the viola; at eight he rode a full-grown horse. Because he was an excellent shot, revelling in the outdoor life and less affected by heat and cold than his contemporaries, he was admired both by the Jacobites and the Italians.

Brimful of energy, Charles was eager for action, and the year before his mother's death, 1734, he had had a taste of it when his cousin the Duke of Liria invited him to join the forces laying siege to Gaeta, the old Roman port between Rome and Naples. The fourteen-year-old Prince got himself into the front lines and behaved with restraint and calm, earning the approval of all around him. During the next two years, while in mourning for his mother, Charles was desperate at being inactive and rode and hunted harder than ever.

In the spring of 1737 James decided his son must go further afield, and allowed him to make a tour of the northern Italian cities—Bologna, Parma, Piacenza, Genoa, Milan, Venice, Padua, Ferrara and Florence—suitably accompanied and travelling

---

[6] BL Add. MSS 34 638, fo. 247, quoted by A. Shield and A. Lang, *The King Over the Water* (1977).

under the title of Count of Albany. His tutor Murray wrote back to the King that on social occasions the Prince could not enjoy the dancing with moderation, but overheated himself 'monstrously', and could not be got to bed before 3 a.m. Murray was surprised, however, at the charm and tact Charles could display when he chose to, especially to older people. Though the Doge of Venice had not intended to receive him, in fact he was given every honour there—which offended the British and resulted in the expulsion of the Venetian envoy from London. The Italians everywhere were captivated by Charles's good looks and social charm; at a meeting in Venice with the Elector of Bavaria, Charles dealt with the 'loaded' questions gracefully, so Murray reported, and when congratulated on his conduct at Gaeta, modestly disclaimed any acts of heroism. When the party returned to Rome at the end of July, Charles was firm in his belief in his destiny as head of a restored Stuart monarchy in Britain.

In 1740 the death of the Emperor Charles VI, and the accession of his daughter, Maria Theresa, led to the attempted dismembering of the Hapsburg empire and eventually to war in Europe. This political situation seemed to offer hopes to the Jacobites, who met at Edinburgh and formed an association binding themselves to restore the House of Stuart, provided the French landed sufficient arms and troops in Scotland. In 1743 at the Battle of Dettingen a superior French force was routed by the English, Hanoverian and Austrian troops. Louis XV, furious, agreed to do all in his power to aid an invasion of England, timed to coincide with a rising in Scotland, to reinstate the Stuarts. A large fleet assembled at the French Channel ports under Admiral de Roquefeuille, and 15,000 troops were brought together under Marshal Saxe.

It was now time to summon Charles from Rome to Paris. A false passport supplied by the Spanish Ambassador in Rome enabled him to give the spies of Sir Horace Mann, the British Envoy in Florence, the slip crossing Tuscany. At the small marble port of Marina di Carrara he managed to get a boat to sail to Genoa, where he rested for thirty-six hours, then sailed to Antibes. The same evening, 29 January 1744, he set out to ride with his friends to Paris, taking the name of Graham. Now he was on his own, a leader in his own right. Meanwhile, he was meeting many of his followers, and striving to learn, as his father had done, how to cope with the divisions among them.

The story of the 1745 rebellion is well known, and in any case outside the scope of this chapter on the Stuarts' Tuscan connection. It is enough to say that throughout the campaign—in which at one point the Scots army penetrated as far south as Derby before, lacking the promised French support, it was forced to retreat and eventually, on 15 April 1746, went down to bloody defeat on the field of Culloden—Charles behaved with exemplary courage and enterprise. From the time he first landed on Eriskay in the Hebrides, wearing the disguise of an abbot, and for nearly all the time he was in Scotland, he led a very rough life, often sleeping in dirty and wet clothes on damp heather, sometimes without having eaten. He was at his best roughing it with his men, whom he never asked to do what he was not prepared to do himself; and he seemed to be none the worse physically for the complete change in the conditions of his life. He was always cheerful, moreover, and, when required, turned on his own particular charm which rarely failed to win him followers.

Even after Culloden, when he was a fugitive, being passed from hand to hand and from house to house in the west of Scotland, dogged by the Hanoverian troops who were searching for him, Charles had an abiding, almost childlike faith that he would be helped; and that he would escape. In the end he was proved right, for the French, though they had not supported him in his moments of victory, had no intention of allowing him to fall into the hands of the British government. Though three or four attempts to find him and get him aboard a ship had failed, after five months of hiding he was eventually taken off by the *Prince de Conti*, transferred to *L'Heureux*, and landed on the coast of Brittany.

Charles proceeded to Paris, knowing that the help he needed to gain the throne could only now come from France or Spain. Ten days after his return, the Prince who a short time ago had been a hunted man dressed in sodden rags, paid a visit to King Louis XV wearing a suit of rose-coloured velvet with waistcoat of gold brocade, all his orders and decorations, diamonds flashing from the cockade of his three-cornered hat and on the buckles of his high-heeled shoes. The King received him courteously, and the Queen, who was Polish and had been a close friend of his mother, welcomed him warmly; yet no help was forthcoming.

The impatient Charles then turned to Spain, whither he went secretly, but the King and Queen asked him to withdraw from Madrid, giving him a sum of money to help him out of his difficulties. A further blow came in the spring of 1747, when his brother Henry, seeing no future for himself in Charles's entourage, without consulting him accepted Pope Benedict XIV's offer to create him a Cardinal. Charles was so angry that for many years he refused to hear Henry's name mentioned, or to go to Rome.

Single-minded as he had been in fighting for his throne, Charles succumbed easily to the pleasures of the sophisticated French court. He took a mistress, the Princess de Talmond, and passed the year 1748 in purely social activity, at the opera, the theatre, and attending balls at which he was the darling of the public. But under the peace of Aix-la-Chapelle France could no longer give him a haven. Louis XV offered him an allowance if he would leave peaceably; when he refused, he had to be unceremoniously and forcibly ejected from France. He went to Avignon for a time, where the papal authorities made life agreeable for him, then travelled about Europe. But for the next two years, when writing to his father, he concealed his whereabouts.

Charles had been fond of the girl who waited on him at Bannockburn, Clementina Walkinshaw, niece of his host there, Sir Hugh Paterson, and at some time between 1750 and 1753 he sent for her. Though not a beauty, Clementina gave him the sympathy and affection he needed at this time. At first they lived happily together, although the Jacobites were suspicious of her loyalty: her sister was in the household of the Princess of Wales in London, but no evidence of communication between the two was ever discovered. On 29 October 1753, Charles's only child, a daughter, was born and baptized Charlotte at Liège.

Mother and child thereafter accompanied him on his renewed

wanderings through Europe, but by now Charles was drinking heavily and there were ugly scenes, when apparently he maltreated Clementina. Finally, in 1760, whilst the ailing James and those around him were trying to persuade Charles to pay a visit to his father in Rome, Clementina planned and carried out her escape. Taking her seven-year-old child in a coach, she fled from Charles in Bouillon. She wrote at length to James to justify her action: 'Your Royalle Highness cannot be surprised at my having taken partty when you consider one repeated bad treatment I have matte with these eight years past, and the Dealy risque of loosing my life . . .',[7] adding a touching postscript vowing that no one had given her the smallest help in escaping, so that blame should not fall 'on innocent people'.

Charles was in a fury. He might not have missed Clementina, but he had been an adoring father, and at once tried desperately but unsuccessfully to have them tracked down. His father wrote, trying to reason with him; Clementina had wished to leave him for some time, he said, to stifle criticism and to give her daughter a Christian education, which was not possible in the sort of 'ambulatory' life Charles was leading. She had written to him, James, 'to implore my Protection, and to seek a subsistance for herself and her Daughter'.[8] This brought a further outburst of rage from Charles, who could not forgive his father for making his support of Charlotte and her mother conditional upon their living apart from Charles. The fact was James could not reconcile himself to his son living openly with a mistress. Charles, for his part, contributed nothing to the education of his daughter. He did not reply to Clementina's letters and she never saw him again.

James was in decline. In 1754 he had suffered a stroke, which cost him the sight of one eye and the use of one hand, and from which he never fully recovered; ten years later he was bedridden. However, it was only when he was evidently dying that Henry, Cardinal York, was able to persuade his brother Charles to set out for Rome to see him. The end came while he was *en route*; the 'Old Chevalier' died peacefully on 1 January 1766. What

---

[7] Letter of 8 September 1760, Stuart Letters 403/42/43.
[8] ibid.

James had longed for all his life was given by Pope Clement XIII at his death: for the royal funeral at St Peter's a crown was placed on his head, and in his hands the orb and sceptre; the coffin bore the royal seal.

Charles did not reach Rome until after the funeral, no doubt preferring to make his entrance when he was already a king. He made overtures of friendship to his brother, the Cardinal, from whom he had been so long estranged, but despite Henry's efforts the Pope refused to recognize him as King Charles III. Clement XIII did, however, put the matter before the College of Cardinals; but, as Horace Mann (claiming to have influenced the decision) wrote on 21 January 1766 to his friend Horace Walpole, 'I have now the satisfaction, Sir, to acquaint you, that in the Congregation of Cardinals held at Rome, to consult about the present Pretender, it has been determined in the negative.'[9]

Charles had hoped none the less to be accorded the respect due to a royal person in Rome. But the Romans regarded him as a foreigner and treated him as such, under his title of Count of Albany. His circumstances had eased, since he now had the pension from the Pope of 12,000 crowns which his brother had made over to him and, as well, all that James had left him in his will. He still hunted, and went out in society. At this period his bouts of drinking seem to have been irregular; in the summer of 1770, however, he left for Pisa on the advice of his doctors to take the treatment of the Baths. There he gambled for several nights, and one day, according to Mann, 'touched for the King's evil', as his father had done, a few 'low' persons who had scrofula. He continued on to Florence, where the Grand Duke of Tuscany, nervous of Britain's disapproval, ordered that he should be ignored. Charles, who was nothing if not stubborn, decided thereupon to settle in Florence. His friends tried to dissuade him, but it was not until his brother, who had power over his finances, intervened, that he returned to Rome. On 17 August 1771 Horace Mann noted that 'the late Pretender's son is removed to Siena where he proposes to stay some time'.[10]

---

[9] *Decline of the Last Stuarts*, ed. Lord Mahon (Roxburghe Club, 1843).
[10] ibid.

The idea of a marriage for Charles seemed to come from the French, who doubtless wished the Stuart line to be carried on in order to upset the English. The bride proposed was Louise of Stolberg, whose father had been killed at the Battle of Leuthen in 1757, fighting for the Empress Maria Theresa against Frederick the Great, and whose mother was dependent on the charity of the Empress. Louise, nearly twenty, was the eldest of four girls; one younger sister had already found a husband. She had been educated at a convent where daughters of the nobility were actually prepared for matrimony; limited dowries had to be provided, and husbands were chosen for the girls without consultation. All that Louise can have known about Charles was his romantic attempt to take the throne of Britain twenty-seven years before. She liked the idea of being regarded as a queen, and of financial security. It was reported to Charles that she was pretty, a little plump, with a fine bust and very red lips, with excellent teeth. This last point must have pleased him, since he associated good health with good teeth; what interested him even more was the annual pension of 40,000 crowns offered by the French on his marriage.

Rumour in Italy had it that the marriage was to take place at Macerata, near Ancona, and many English visitors arrived in the town; some attended the wedding. The Marefoschi family placed their palace and private chapel at the Prince's disposal; and the Bishop of Macerata and Tolentino officiated at the ceremony. The marriage document, which has been preserved, was signed 'Charles III of Great Britain, France and Ireland' and 'Louise R'. A plaque on the chapel wall commemorates the wedding which for some reason took place on Good Friday, the saddest day in the Christian year. On the following day, Holy Saturday, there was a performance by the Academy of Music, and on Easter Sunday the newlyweds left for Rome. Many English, invited or not, rode back with them. They stayed a night on the way with Charles's friend Count Spada, and Louise, far from being the unsophisticated young girl sometimes portrayed, shocked the Countess by wearing rouge and showing her hostess how to apply it.

Having the wedding outside Rome had saved a lot of money;

and though no official entry into the city had been planned, by the time they reached the outskirts of Rome, the crowd awaiting them had grown quite large. One coach bore a special envoy from Cardinal York, who, though relations between the brothers had remained cool, was delighted to have Charles married. Henry hoped that Louise would restrain Charles from drinking, though Horace Mann prophesied privately, 'She will be condemned to live alone with him, for he is drunk half the day and mad the other half.'[11]

The marriage began well, however. Henry called on the bride bringing magnificent wedding presents, including a gold lace court dress and a diamond-studded snuff box containing a draft on his banker for 40,000 crowns. Though the present Pope, Clement XIV, like his predecessor refused to recognize Charles as King Charles III, and the papal guard round the Palazzo Muti had been withdrawn and the royal arms over the doorway taken down, in other ways the couple were shown every respect and courtesy. Within the palace each had to be addressed as 'Your Majesty', and Louise received visitors with the royal prerogative that she did not have to return the visits. Charles enjoyed showing his wife the sights of Rome, wearing his blue ribbon of the Garter wherever he went.

Louise, fair, elegant in the French manner, and amiable, became known as the 'Queen of Hearts', and was not averse to having young men flirt with or even fall in love with her. When a handsome young Englishman, William Coke (afterwards Earl of Leicester), on the Grand Tour, prolonged his stay in Rome to talk to her about culture, she paid him the great compliment of commissioning the artist Pompeo Batoni to paint his portrait, now in the possession of the Earl of Leicester at Holkham Hall. Back in England, Coke was thought by Horace Walpole, gossiping to Mann in Florence, to be 'quite in love with the Pretender's Queen'. However, Coke married Jane Dutton; and when years later his eldest daughter, Lady Andover, was in Florence, Louise called on her to reminisce about her father.

Another of Louise's admirers who was often at the Palazzo Muti in 1774 was Karl Victor von Bonstettin, who later became

11 ibid.

a member of Madame de Stael's circle. Bonstettin was twenty-nine (her husband was more than fifty), and not surprisingly Louise found it enjoyable to flirt with him as well as to discuss books. He remembered her teasing and that 'her natural gaiety was somewhat laced with malice, her malice was sometimes friendship, or better than that'. Somewhat strangely (or perhaps because he was less prejudiced than other observers), he described the Prince as a 'tall thin man, good-hearted and talkative. He was friendly towards me because I was practically the only man received in his house who understood English well and spoke it when necessary. He enjoyed describing his adventures . . . .'[12] But those adventures had all taken place long before Bonstettin was born.

In 1775 the Pope's Jubilee celebrations drove Charles, out of pride, to leave Rome, for he could have attended the festivities only as Count of Albany and not as a king. They went north and stayed a while in Siena, where the welcome of some hundreds of people on the bridge as they passed somewhat assuaged his tormented vanity, and where Louise was happy because Bonstettin was also in Siena. And there were other young men: the inveterate gossip, Sir Horace Mann, remarking that same year that 'a Mr Danby, son of a rich Yorkshire gentleman' was to be married to 'the eldest Miss Seymour', said he was sure the Countess of Albany would be upset because she had grown fond of Danby. Charles, it seems, allowed his wife these discreet flirtations—discreet enough, that is, that the paternity of a possible heir would never be disputed—but she was never for long allowed out of his sight.

Charles had decided by then to settle in Florence, away from the Vatican, where he felt it would be cheaper to maintain his little court. His friend Prince Corsini offered him a small palazzo on Via del Prato, used by the Corsini family only at the height of the summer, whilst he was looking around for a house of his own, and he and Louise actually remained there for two years. The Corsini family still possess the yellow diamond given them by Prince Charles in gratitude, and a miniature of two small red-headed boys—obviously himself and his brother Henry. The

12 C. V. Bonstettin, *Souvenirs* (Geneva, 1831).

Geoffrey Chaucer, as portrayed in *De Regimine Principium* (1411–12), a work by his friend Thomas Hoccleve.

The rigours of the road towards the end of the 18th century, as suggested by William Bunbury.

AENEAS SILVIVS A BASILIENSI CONCILIO IN VLTERIOREM·BRITANI

Aeneas Silvius Piccolomini, later Pope Pius II, being received by King
James I of Scotland: a scene from Pinturicchio's fresco in the Cathedral
Library at Siena.

A detail—the Nativity—from the cope of Pope Pius II, embroidered in
England and described by the Pope as excelling 'all others in Christendom in
its work and craftsmanship'.

The hall of Salimbeni Castle, Siena, now the headquarters of the Monte de Paschi di Siena, the first modern-style bank in the world, established in 1472.

palazzo is now the home of Prince Tomaso Corsini, whose grandfather acquired the house next to it, joining the two and levelling up the floors. But in Charles's day the house was on different levels, with steps up and down, which must have been awkward for the Prince, who was drinking heavily again.

Though his health was declining, he remained keen on exercise, and walked with Louise daily in the Cascine Gardens near by. When the young Duke of Hamilton, making the Grand Tour in the company of his physician Dr Moore, passed the Prince and his wife, Dr Moore thought that the Prince looked at the Duke as if thinking 'our ancestors were better acquainted'.[13] Moore described Louise as 'a beautiful woman', and had heard that she was 'lively, intelligent and agreeable'—though in fact she objected so strongly to taking these walks in the month of June at the time of day when the heat overcame her, that she refused to speak to her husband, writing cold scornful letters to him instead. Things were not going well between them. Horace Mann reported that 'she behaves to him with all the attention, nay tenderness, that is possible. He never quits her.' But she was, in fact, a prisoner. Charles had always been a jealous person, and he had shown the same possessiveness with Clementina Walkinshaw when they lived together. Louise undoubtedly gave him cause for jealousy, and it was perhaps no wonder that 'all the avenues to her room, excepting through his own, are barricaded. The reason given for this, that the succession may never be dubious.'[14]

As she saw few people, Louise was glad of her enforced visits to the theatre. Horace Mann wrote that the Prince

will not stay at home. He goes every evening to the theatre, where he sits in the corner box, in a drowsy posture, but is frequently obliged, by sickness at his stomach, to retire to the common and much frequented corridors. I have seen him in that condition, assisted by two servants, all the others that attend there fly from such a nuisance.[15]

[13] John Moore, *Memoirs* (1820).
[14] Dr J. Doran, *'Mann' and Manners at the Court of Florence, 1740–1786* (1876), vol. II.
[15] ibid.

When Charles had difficulty in sitting upright, Mann reported, a couch was made for his box, so that he could stretch out, and on it he slept for the greater part of the evening. It must have been sad for the Florentines to see how the once young, brave and dashing Prince, who had almost won back his father's throne, had deteriorated.

Charles had meanwhile settled on the house he wanted to buy —the Palazzo Guadagni, built by the architect Gherardo Silvano in the mid-seventeenth century. Its purchase involved him in litigation with the rich Earl Cowper, owner of the Villa Palmieri, where he gave lavish parties to which, after their suit, Charles and Louise were not invited. There was difficulty also over the contract for the palazzo, since Charles wished to sign *Carolus Rex*, which would not have been acceptable in law. But at length the house became his, and he placed in front of it the great shield with the armorial bearings of Great Britain and France, and the date of his succession on his father's death, 1766. A weather vane on the roof bore the royal cipher 'C.R.' and the date 1777, until it was removed a few years ago.

It was said that the San Clemente family, Neapolitans, descendants of an old Florentine family, who bought the house soon after the Prince's death, had retained a fresco incorporating his Stuart tartan; but the building has been much altered and in the painting over of walls and ceilings any trace of a tartan has disappeared. On the ceiling of the entrance hall, however, from the centre of which hangs an ornate candelabra of wrought iron, partly gilded and topped by a crown, is a fresco of two maidens floating upwards with cherubic angels above in the clouds. One of the maidens wears a crown and holds in her right hand an up-lifted sword and in her left the scales of justice. Was this specially painted for Charles as a reference to his just claim to the throne? Perhaps the fate of its Stuart owner infected the house, for the Palazzo Guadagni was reputed to harbour evil spirits. Once when an elderly Bishop of the San Clemente family was saying mass in the chapel, the evil spirits seemed to have invaded him, and he kept motioning them away with his hands. But the spirits apparently did not depart, and later owners of the house are said to have left it in despair.

★   ★   ★

Despite their splendid new house and the outward trappings of royalty, Louise was unhappy in Florence. But she had borne her disappointing married life remarkably well until she met the poet and dramatist Vittoria Alfieri, the lover who was destined to change everything for her. Count Alfieri, son of a noble Piedmontese family, was a man supremely conscious of his own importance, who had had love affairs with other married women but continued to love best himself and his horses. At his first meeting with Louise and her husband in the Uffizi Gallery, her 'exceedingly dark eyes', blond hair and white skin had attracted him.

Charles liked the young poet and did not discourage his daily visits to the Palazzo Guadagni, until one day he began to suspect he was being cuckolded. Anger rose in him and, very drunk on St Andrew's night, 30 November 1780, he made, according to his wife, an attack on her. Louise decided she could bear him no longer, and a plan was worked out for her escape. A woman friend breakfasted at the Palazzo Guadagni, and went with Louise to the convent of the Little White Nuns on the pretext of seeing some exquisite needlework. Charles insisted on accompanying them in the carriage and was following them up to the door of the convent when Louise and her companion disappeared inside and the door was shut in his face. He realized that he had been tricked, but he dared not try to force his way into such a house.

Louise, however, had no intention of remaining in the convent. She cleverly wrote to her brother-in-law Henry, confessing her flight and asking his help in getting her into a convent in Rome. Henry, who had always deplored Charles's drunkenness and felt sympathy with a wife forced to endure it constantly, immediately approached the Pope on her behalf. It was arranged that Louise was to go into the convent of the Ursulines in Rome, where his mother, Clementina, had made a temporary stay before her marriage, and where Louise would be well treated according to her rank. The Cardinal hoped the separation might induce Charles to mend his ways and that there might be a reconciliation. Louise, who had arranged her escape without a mention of Alfieri, did not for her part wish a formal separation from Charles until she had financial security, which would depend on her presumed innocence.

Count Orsini tried to put Charles's side of the story to the Pope but was snubbed. Early in 1781, Louise left the convent, with the Pope's permission, for a luxurious apartment in the Cardinal's palace, the Cancelleria. Henry himself preferred living at Frascati, in the Albano hills, of which he had been made Bishop in 1761, and in his palace in Rome she would be free to entertain and to accept invitations. Meanwhile she had arranged her financial prospects very cleverly, having gained half the pension of 12,000 crowns which the Pope had been giving to her husband.

Alfieri had gone to Naples, whence he wrote passionate letters to her, but by May 1781 he was back in Rome. For the next two years, comfortably installed in the Villa Strozzi near the Baths of Diocletian, he wrote all day and visited Louise every evening. He was on friendly terms with the Cardinal, and Louise used her influence to have his play *Antigone* put on in the Duke of Grimaldi's private theatre. Louise had been adroit: she had established herself in a new life with a lover near by, had secured for herself a good income, and no social stigma had attached to her.

Then, early in 1783, news reached Rome that the Count of Albany had been near to death and had been administered the last sacraments. His breathing was laboured and his legs so swollen it seemed he would never walk again even if he survived. Cardinal York hastened to Florence, but Charles had recovered by the time his brother arrived, and was able at last to pour out his side of the story to the Cardinal. It should be known, Charles declared, that Louise had a lover, yet no one had listened to Orsini in Rome, and, worst of all, his own brother had accepted all Louise's stories. Henry was much annoyed to find he had been fooled, and, to make matters worse, on returning to Rome he learned that the situation was well known. He rushed to the Pope with the whole story, and Pius VI angrily issued a mandate, compelling Alfieri to leave Rome at once. The poet retreated to Siena; in the meantime Louise wrote with consummate tact to the Cardinal that she had taken his advice and persuaded Alfieri to leave Rome.

As part of a plot in one of his many tragedies, Alfieri had used the story that Charles ill-treated his wife. The Cardinal now published an account of Louise's intrigues with Alfieri, but to a certain extent Louise was still triumphant. In 1784 she secured a legal separation from Charles, brought about by King Gustavus III of Sweden, who was travelling in Italy for his health; the King sympathized deeply with the Prince, for he himself was unhappily married. The separation agreement stipulated that she was to receive no income from the House of Stuart; instead, she would have the pension from France provided for in her marriage contract, but which in spite of petitions she had never in fact received. She went to Paris in May 1785, to settle her financial affairs, and after discussion and examination of these Louis XV granted her her pension.

In Paris Louise found she could entertain and hold, as it were, a minor court, surrounding herself with the royal emblem on her silver and porcelain, and that she could form the beginnings of a small literary-social salon. To be beautiful and of high rank, she observed, gave one a certain degree of power, and she was still young enough at thirty-four to enjoy the Parisian scene. Her liaison with Alfieri continued.

Meanwhile in Florence Charles was ill and lonely, and made a will in favour of his only child, Charlotte, daughter of Clementina Walkinshaw. When he recovered, feeling he needed someone to love and care for him, he decided to send for the thirty-year-old Charlotte. She arrived in Florence from France in the autumn of 1784.

Charlotte had always been proud of her ancestry, and was determined not to be pushed into obscurity if she could help it. Her mother had given her as good a convent education as she could afford on the pension she had from the French and from James (though that was halved by Cardinal York after James's death). Through the years she had written regular if rather obsequious and complaining letters to her father, to which he did not reply. As early as 1755 he had forbidden her to marry. She and her mother had come to Rome at the time of his marriage to Louise, but it was hardly the moment to approach him for recognition, and they returned to Paris without meeting him. At that time, of course, he was hoping for the eveutual birth of a legitimate Stuart heir. Charlotte, meanwhile, had been forbidden to marry; but while officially residing at the convent at Meaux she had become the mistress of Prince de Rohan, Archbishop of Bordeaux, by whom she had three children, two girls and a boy. Her mother now became responsible for the children, and Charlotte wrote regularly for news of them, her letters providing a record of her years in Italy with her father.

She made a good impression on the Florentines. 'She is gay, lively, very affable,' wrote Horace Mann, 'and has the behaviour of a well-bred Frenchwoman, without assuming the least distinction among our Ladies on account of her new dignity.' In order to give her a position superior to that of his ex-wife, Charles had created her Duchess of Albany, after she was legitimized by him; and he held a ceremony to confer on her the Order of the Thistle. As Mann reported,

> The new Duchess has appeared at the Theatres (which were crowded on her account) with all her father's jewels, which are very fine. He . . . had permission to line the Boxes as he pleased. That in the Great Theatre is hung with Crimson Damask. In the other Theatre it is yellow Damask. The Count is much pleased with this distinction. . . . We have heard that the King of France has legitimated her so far as to enable her to inherit what her father possesses in France; and (it is said) she was received in quality of Duchesse at the Court, and had the Tabouret.[16]

In March 1785 Charlotte and her father paid a short visit to Pisa, taking a suite of thirty people, and there she was presented to the King and Queen of Naples.

There is no doubt that Charlotte brought some happiness to her father's last years. She had persuaded him to pay off her debts, and later in 1785 managed to bring about a reconciliation between him and Cardinal York. Charles announced his intention of returning to Rome, to spend the winter in the Palazzo Muti where he had been born, returning to Florence in the spring. The Florentines held an immense fête in their honour, attended

[16] ibid.

by all the Tuscan nobility, to wish them *bon voyage*. They stopped *en route* in Siena, where Charlotte wrote that her father had never been so happy or so amiable, even though he had been sitting twelve hours in the carriage. From Viterbo she wrote again that her father was still full of gaiety, and that all honours were being shown to them in the Papal States.

Over the next two years they spent much time in Rome. Though Charles resented the affection that evidently grew up between his daughter and his brother, the Cardinal, there were compensations—as when the Pope, to Charles's enormous satisfaction, granted to him, as to his late father, the use of the Royal Tribuna in St Peter's; they took possession of it on Christmas Day 1785.

In the year 1787 both father and daughter were ill, though Charles insisted on attending all the balls and fêtes as usual, and Charlotte wrote of receiving in the room the nobility and distinguished travellers then in Rome, including the Duke of Buccleuch from Scotland. On 23 January 1788, however, Charles had a slight stroke, losing his speech, and leaving half his body paralysed, and he died a week later, on 30 January 1788, in the Palazzo Muti.

Six altars were erected in the antechamber of the palace and masses were said continually for the next thirty hours. The Irish Franciscans of Saint Isidore, who had administered the last rites to the Prince, were the only ones permitted to enter the room where his body lay. A cast of his face was taken, and the body was then embalmed and placed in a cypress wood coffin, on which an inscription read *Carolus III Magnae Britanniae rex*. As the Pope would not permit Charles to be buried in St Peter's, as his father James Edward had been, his brother Henry gave him a royal funeral in his own bishopric of Frascati, which was attended by many, both British and Italian. The coffin, covered by a magnificent pall embroidered with the arms of Great Britain, was placed on a large catafalque, erected on the steps of the nave of the cathedral, with the crown, sceptre and sword, as well as his Orders of Chivalry, including those of the Garter and the Thistle. When the Cardinal began to intone the Office for the Dead, his voice was broken with emotion.

After the funeral the Cardinal issued a manifesto asserting his hereditary right as a Stuart to the British Crown under the title of Henry IX. Nine years later Charles's remains were removed to Rome and buried in the crypt of St Peter's. But the Hanoverians continued to reign unhindered.

Charlotte did not have long to enjoy the position in society which her father and uncle had taken pains to establish for her. She decided to sell the palazzo in Florence and its contents, in order to pay off Charles's debts, find the money for Louise's pension, and various smaller legacies, and have enough for herself and her mother. The Pope had granted her the continued use of the Royal Tribuna in St Peter's, a privilege of which everyone was jealous, and she used this as an excuse for staying on in Rome. She wrote to her mother that she was to use the royal arms of England as her father had, and she continued the ceremonial of royalty: visitors were 'presented' to her. She decided to use only the livery of the House of Stuart, as her uncle's servants did, unless she could declare herself heiress to the throne of Great Britain, and for that, she wrote in all seriousness, an Act of Parliament would be required.

Her situation seems always to have been dominated by her financial problems, and her attitude both to her uncle, now sixty-four but still firmly in control of the purse-strings, and to the father of her children, the Prince Archbishop of Bordeaux. Obviously her royal status in Italy depended upon her total discretion about those children. Her 'ami' talked of coming to Rome, which she did not wish. In April of 1789, worried about the political situation in Paris, she suggested that her mother go to Switzerland with the children. If they were nearer, the Cardinal might allow her to visit her mother. Yet she did not find a way to see them. In her will, made just before she died, she names her uncle, Cardinal York, her heir; an annual payment to be made to her mother, legacies to each member of her staff, but no mention of her children.

That summer of 1789 Charlotte planned a two months' journey for her health, which was obviously deteriorating, and had some difficulty in getting her uncle to agree to it. At Loreto, the richness and beauty of the Madonna and her jewels impressed her; at Ancona she delighted in the sea air and the view. She died in Bologna, in the house of a friend, on 17 November 1789, and was buried without ceremony, according to her own wishes, in the Bolognese church of San Biagio (later destroyed by the French). A memorial service was held for her in Frascati, and her uncle formally announced the death of 'his beloved niece' to foreign courts and to friends.

Henry, Cardinal York, lived on for almost twenty years. Though said to be one of the richest of the Cardinals, in February 1798 his life seemed to be in ruins, when he had to fly before the invading French troops, and lost everything. He went first to Naples, then to Messina, and from thence to Venice, arriving there very ill and almost penniless in 1799. Sir John Coxe Hippisly, who had been a semi-official representative of the British government at the papal court of Pius VI, appealed to George II of England on his behalf, and a pension of £4,000 per annum was paid to him for the rest of his life. In return he left some of the British crown jewels still in his possession to George III, including the Scottish coronation ring, and the Orders of chivalry.

Henry returned to Rome when the French withdrew, and three years later, as senior Cardinal, became Dean of the Sacred College and Bishop of Ostia and Velletri. He died on 13 January 1807, and was buried in the Grotte Vaticane of St Peter's, in an urn bearing the title of *Henry IX*. The great Canova was commissioned by the Pope to design and sculpt a monument to the royal Stuarts for St Peter's; a contribution was made to it by George III. The State Archives of the Stuart line were presented to Pope Pius VII, and sent to the Prince Regent in England, who placed them in the Royal Library at Windsor Castle.

At the north end of the Piazza dei Santi Apostoli in Rome in the small courtyard of a shabby baroque building once the Palazzo Muti but now housing a restaurant and offices, is a plaque on the left-hand wall bearing this inscription:

ABITO QUESTO PALAZZO
ENRICO DUC POI CARDINALE DI YORK
CHE FIGLIO SUPERSTITE DI GIACOMO III D'INGHILTERRA
PRESE IL NOME D'ENRICO IX

The Divine Country

IN LUI NELL'ANNO MDCCCVII
S'ESTINSE LA DINASTIA DE STUARDI.[17]

There was one other survivor of the Stuart connection. With the death of Charles, Louise, Countess of Albany, was now free to marry her poet; but by this time it seems doubtful that she wanted to. Alfieri, for his part, though needing her occasional presence, apparently had no great desire for matrimony. Over the years he had had affairs with other women, of which Louise had not been unaware though she showed no signs of jealousy. They had gone on leading their separate lives, writing letters and meeting secretly from time to time, often at Colmar. Louise took herself and her special position very seriously indeed, and after the deaths of her husband and later of his daughter Charlotte, had a room in her apartments fitted out with a chair of state, covered in a canopy emblazoned with the royal arms of Great Britain. All her servants addressed her as 'Your Majesty', and an English visitor, Sir Nathaniel Wraxall, observed that 'Every piece of plate, down to the very teaspoons, was ornamented in a similar manner' with the royal arms.

In the spring of 1791 Louise and Alfieri visited England, where her relative, Lady Ailesbury, arranged for her to be received at court. Horace Mann received an eye-witness account of the occasion from his friend Walpole ('The King talked to her a great deal, but always about her passage, the sea, and general topics; the Queen in the same way but less'). Walpole was also invited to a reception given for Louise by Lady Ailesbury. He was disappointed: 'Not a rag of royalty about her. She has good eyes and teeth, but I think can have had not more beauty than remains, except youth. She is civil and easy but German and ordinary.'[18] Louise's presence in London with her lover, Alfieri, caused no stir at all.

They returned to Paris, but were driven out by the Revolution, and lost all their possessions, furniture, library and horses. They were declared *émigrés* and were lucky to be the first two

---

[17] There lived in this building Henry, Duke, later Cardinal, of York, who, surviving son of James III of England, took the name of Henry IX. In him in the year 1807 the Stuart dynasty became extinct.
[18] Doran, op. cit.

foreigners allowed out of France after the arrest of the King. They then returned to Italy, where Louise had lived for twenty years, but after Paris she thought Florence provincial, and Italian women spiteful. She considered settling in Pisa, but it was apparently more expensive than Florence, and as Alfieri wrote, Louise was used to living in state. Late in 1793 they found a house, the Casa Gianfigliazzi, near the bridge of Santa Trinitá, facing south across the Arno. Louise was somewhat lonely, and spent a great deal of time reading and writing letters. She was little interested in politics, even at this time when Napoleon was making history so close to Florence. What she missed most was friendship with someone from the land of her birth, and the young French painter, François Xavier-Fabre, filled this need. Though he was fourteen years younger than she, he became her close friend, and later, it was said, during Alfieri's last years, her lover. To Fabre posterity owes paintings both of Louise and Alfieri.

When Alfieri died at fifty-three, in October 1803, Fabre was at Louise's side and he never left her thereafter. In 1809 she was recalled to Paris by Napoleon, who, knowing that Alfieri had hated France, mistrusted the influence of her and her friends. Fabre accompanied her to Paris, where she was received by the Emperor, who wanted to know if she had ever had a son by Charles Edward! Napoleon apparently decided she was harmless and she was free to return to Florence. Louise was anxious to see the large marble monument to Alfieri which Canova had sculpted for the church of Santa Croce; she found it 'grandiose without being gigantic'. Her own monument, erected by Fabre in the same church, proudly displays the royal arms of England!

Having failed to produce a Stuart heir, Louise's real claim to fame was the twenty-five years she spent with Alfieri. Henry James described her curious ability to 'associate sentimentally with three diverse figures—a disqualified sovereign, an Italian dramatist and a bad French painter.'[19] She died of dropsy in 1824 at her home in Florence.

---

[19] *A Little Town in France* (1900).

V

'Travelling Boys' and *Cicisbei:* The Florence of Sir Horace Mann

'THERE are few private assemblies,' wrote an English visitor to Florence in 1776; 'before Sir Horace Mann came there was not any: but he has been of great use in teaching them how to live; his table is elegant, and his polite manners please everybody: none more so than his own countrymen.'[1] Sir Horace Mann, His Britannic Majesty's Envoy to the Tuscan court, would hardly have been flattered by this comment, though he would have basked in the compliment to his lifestyle, of which he was most particular. He regarded his role in Florence as much more important than the mere introduction of the manners of the self-assured British into Italian social life. Yet this ambitious, scandal-loving social climber did as much as anyone to shape the unique relationship that existed between the United Kingdom and Tuscany. And because this fastidious bachelor, with his womanish eye for nuance and solecism in the everyday behaviour of a sophisticated and elegant society, was also a prodigious letter-writer, the stream of his daily gossip to his young friend Horace Walpole, filling several volumes, tells us more about life in eighteenth-century Florence than almost any other source.

Vain and affected, always impeccably dressed, more than somewhat effeminate and never in the most robust health, Horace Mann (Sir Horace after 1755, when he succeeded to his father's baronetcy) was what we would today call a career diplomat. He went to Florence in 1738 in a comparatively humble post as assistant to Charles Fane, the British representative there, on the recommendation of the then Prime Minister, Sir Robert

---

[1] Lady A. Miller, *Letters from Italy*, vol. I (1776).

Walpole. Mann worked hard to consolidate his position, and in 1740 took over Fane's duties, with the title of Resident; from then until his death in 1786 he was a key figure in British–Tuscan diplomatic and social relations, being made Envoy Extraordinary in 1765 and Minister in 1782. His duties were mainly to look after British travellers and residents in Tuscany, and to keep a close watch on the movements of the Stuart Pretenders to the British throne, who were then living in Italy. In addition he had to protect the interests of British traders at Leghorn in their dealings with the Tuscan government, and to act as liaison officer with the British fleet in the Mediterranean. His brief sometimes involved him in difficult and delicate situations but he did his work conscientiously and skilfully.

In his first years in Florence Mann had to work hard as assistant to the indolent Fane, who was the sort of person, he related, 'who took to his bed for six weeks because the Duke of Newcastle omitted on one occasion the usual prefix "very" to "your humble servant" at the bottom of a letter'. However, in December 1739, shortly before Mann was to take over from Fane, Horace Walpole, youngest son of the Prime Minister, arrived in the city with his friend, the poet Thomas Gray, and life became more interesting. Despite the difference in their ages, an immediate friendship sprang up between the young sprig Walpole, making the Grand Tour at the age of twenty-three, and the thirty-eight-year-old bachelor diplomat.

A young man of Walpole's position would usually have been sent on the Tour in the company of his tutor, often a clergyman, who stood for parental authority. But with characteristic broad-mindedness Sir Robert Walpole had allowed his son to travel with an Etonian school friend of his own age. Both Horace Walpole and Gray had intellectual tastes and both had been in delicate health. Mann found them delightfully different from the usual 'travelling boys' and 'flights of woodcock' sent to complete their education on the Grand Tour, who trespassed on his leisure and frequently abused his hospitality. As the royal arms were above the door of his house, Casa Manetti, in the Via Santo Spirito, it was often referred to as the 'King's Arms', and visitors took for granted their right to dine there, to have their letters sent there, and to use it as a coffee house, where one could find the latest English newspapers, which Mann often read aloud to assembled guests. He also maintained a guest-house, Casa Ambrogi, opposite the Pitti Palace, where his visitors were sometimes accommodated.

Though Casa Manetti was one of the centres of social life for members of the leading Florentine families as well as for the British, Mann seems to have run the whole place almost single-handed. He had no housekeeper, and as the British Government did not allow him an assistant, he had only an inefficient Italian secretary, until Horace Walpole, on his return to England, sent out a young clerk who was able also to wait at table. Yet Mann entertained constantly, with assemblies held indoors in winter, and in summer in the garden. One British traveller recalled such an occasion:

> All the appartments on the ground-floor, which is elegantly furnished, were lighted up, and in the garden was a little epitome of Vauxhall. These little conversazione [*sic*] resemble our card-assemblies; and this one was remarkably brilliant, for all the married ladies of fashion in Florence were there.[2]

Mann often complained that his finances were greatly in arrears, but he obviously presented a smooth-running establishment; it would have surprised him to know that Casanova later described him as rich: '*l'idole de Florence, homme riche, aimable, grand amateur des arts et plein de gout.*'[3]

In the winter of 1739-40, when Walpole and Gray arrived in Florence, social life was relatively formal, but when Carnival time came the Florentines celebrated without restraint. Walpole was popular with those he met and lent himself enthusiastically to the festivities. At Casa Manetti one did not need to rise until noon, and the days passed in leisurely fashion. In the evening the whole town gathered at the Ponte Vecchio, lingering in the warm, soft evening air, dining, listening to music, carrying on intrigues. There were also operas, masquerades, assemblies, balls and *conversazioni* in moonlit gardens scented with orange blossom and visited by nightingales. Writing to Walpole later, after he

[2] Alexander Drummond, *Travels through Different Cities* (1754).
[3] *Mémoires*, ed. R. Veze vol. VII (1826).

had returned to England, Mann described an evening like those Walpole had enjoyed:

> There's a very great Cocchiata [a serenade in coaches] tonight on the Terrass of the Corsini house, *Lung' Arno*. Chains are put up at the end of the street, to prevent Coaches approaching, so that the whole town be there, or thereabout, a-foot; 'tis a charming situation, you know, for such a thing; and the night is most favourable, after some of the hottest days, they say, of this or any other summer. Oh, if you were here, I am sure you would be pleased and would be amongst 'em in your long nightgown till break of day. 'Tis made by 12 Cavalieri, set on foot and managed by Abbate Capponi. It begins at 5 hours.[4]

Walpole had not, at first, been impressed by the city itself, and was probably overwhelmed by its plethora of artistic and architectural masterpieces; Gray, on the other hand, was enchanted by the paintings and sculpture and works of art collected by the Medici over the generations, and by the churches and palaces, themselves also full of treasures. But as their visit continued Walpole began to feel more at home. Writing on 25 September 1740 to his cousin Conway, he explained that Florence was rather like a country town where everyone was happily paired and 'nobody hangs or drowns themselves; they are not ready to cut another's throat about elections or parties . . .'[5] Walpole too seems to have found a partner: it was generally assumed that he was the lover of the beautiful Signora Griffoni, whose *cicisbeo* he became, and—perhaps to allay other suspicions—he made no secret of his success with the lady. He approved the fashion of the time whereby a married woman would be escorted by a gentleman of her choice, whilst her husband acted *cicisbeo* to some other lady. Sometimes it was an arrangement of social convenience and friendship, sometimes it involved a sexual relationship.

There was a fly in the ointment, however, in this idyllic city, and that was that Margaret Rolle, who had married Horace's

[4] Dr J. Doran *'Mann' and Manners at the Court of Florence, 1740–1786* (1876), vol. I. Further quotations in this chapter from Mann's letters to Walpole are taken from Doran's two-volume compilation.
[5] *Letters of Horace Walpole*, ed. Paget Toynbee, vol. I (1903).

eldest brother, Lord Robert Walpole (later the Earl of Orford), had settled in Florence. After living with Robert Walpole and bearing him a son, this lady had quarrelled violently with the whole Walpole family, and left England proclaiming her woes wherever she went. Her young brother-in-law Horace detested her, finding her ill-tempered and malicious.

Horace Walpole always expressed a dislike of the priesthood, and the Roman Church was in his mind inseparably linked with the Stuart Pretenders. On 1 February 1740, however, when Pope Clement XII died, he and Gray reluctantly set off for Rome, to witness the Conclave for the election of the new Pope. Walpole missed Mann's company, and the diversions he so readily provided, and was worried by Gray's 'solemn and indefatigable pursuit of learning'. He longed to return to Mann's cool house, but Gray wanted to stay on in Rome. They visited Naples, returning to Rome to find the Conclave still in session; in fact, the new Pope was not elected until six weeks later.

Eventually Walpole's wishes prevailed and they came back to Florence in early July. Walpole settled in as Mann's guest in rooms on the ground floor of the Casa Manetti, which had an open gallery facing the Arno (from some of the windows it was possible to fish in the river, but its course must have altered somewhat since then), and Gray in two small rooms close by. After the brilliant summer the city, now in mourning for the death of the Emperor Charles VII, settled into a quiet routine of gatherings for cards and music. Each Monday Mann had a 'select set, and a sixpenny pharo-table' at Casa Manetti; the Pomfrets had the same on Thursday, and Sir Francis Dashwood a concert every Wednesday.

Gray resented having left Rome for the idle existence of Florence, which he found 'an excellent place to employ one's animal sensations in, but utterly contrary to one's rational powers',[6] as he told his friend and classmate Richard West. The novelty and fascination of travel had at first had a buoyant effect on him, but his natural shyness and melancholy were beginning once again to assert themselves. Gray himself was conscious of

[6] Postscript to letter from Walpole to West, 31 July 1740, quoted in Edmund Gosse, *Gray* (1902); see also the Revd William Mason, *Life and Letters of Thomas Gray* (1774).

this and wrote on 21 April 1741 to West:

> Methinks I ought to send you my picture (for I am no more what I was) . . . you must add then to your former idea two years of age, reasonable quantity of dullness, a great deal of silence, and something that rather resembles, than is, thinking; a confused notion of many strange and fine things that have swum before my eyes for some time, a want of love for general society, indeed an inability to it.[7]

He spent his days in the galleries making detailed notes on all he saw, studied the guidebooks and read Latin authors for historical information; in the libraries he copied musical scores and material from bound manuscripts. Here he wrote most of 'De Principiis Cogitandi' his long Latin poem on the philosophy of Locke, and, also in Latin, farewell poems to the Arno, the groves of Fiesole, and the cypress-lined gardens of the great villas. Despite his discontent while there, after his return to England Gray said that every letter he received from Florence made him desire to return, and whilst walking among the crowds of London he dreamed of the ease and leisure of the Tuscan city.

In Florence in 1741, however, Horace Walpole observed his companion's moody low spirits and lack of sympathy for his own idle, pleasurable life, and reacted with a certain amount of arrogance. He simply felt that Gray was becoming pedantic, and boring. One does not know how soon the tension between the friends became obvious to those in Casa Manetti, but it must have been extremely embarrassing for Mann, who valued them both. Thirty years later, after Gray's death, Walpole took full blame for the breach, writing on 2 March 1773 to the Revd William Mason, who was writing the life of Gray:

> I was too young, too fond of my own diversions, nay I do not doubt, too much intoxicated by indulgence, vanity, and the insolence of my situation as a Prime Minister's son, not to have been inattentive and insensible to the feeling of one I thought below me; of one, I blush to say it, that I knew was obliged to me; of one whom presumption and folly perhaps made me deem not

---

[7] Mason, op. cit.

my superior than in parts; though I have since felt my finite inferiority to him. . . . You will not wonder that with the dignity of his spirit, and the obstinate carelessness of mine, the breach must have grown wider, till we became incompatible.[8]

Outwardly in accord, Walpole and Gray left Florence in the spring of 1741, on the first stage of their journey home. They had stayed with Mann for fifteen months altogether. They stopped at Bologna, where Walpole wrote a thank-you letter to Mann, and enclosed an affectionate farewell letter to Signora Griffoni, which before long was being passed around Florence and pronounced the most beautiful letter it was possible to see. Walpole took back to England a dog, Patapan, which Elisabeth Griffoni had given him as a parting gift, together with her portrait; the latter, though he was later to say that it made his 'beautiful *cicisbea* look like a surly margravine',[9] hung in his bedroom until the end of his life.

The two young Englishmen proceeded to Reggio, where Walpole threw himself into the gaiety of the annual fair. A quarrel must have sprung up, as Gray left for Venice and Walpole remained behind. He fell ill with quinsy and, foolishly, did not consult a doctor until his condition had deteriorated to the point where he was saved only by the timely arrival from Florence of two of Mann's friends. Lord Lincoln and his tutor, the classicist Joseph Spence, sent for the best physician in Reggio, and later for another Florentine friend of Mann's, the invaluable Dr Cocchi. After some hours Walpole's condition improved and Cocchi's report on his return to Florence was a great relief to Mann. He wrote begging Walpole to renew his friendship with Gray, and the two appear to have met. But Gray refused Walpole's offer of financial aid, and Mann had therefore to supply Gray with funds until he could receive a credit from England to cover his return journey. Gray never realized that the money came, in fact from Walpole, and it was not until three years later, in 1744 in England, that the breach between the two was healed.

Meanwhile Horace Walpole, recovered from his illness, had gone on from Venice with Lord Lincoln and Spence. Travelling

[8] *Letters of Horace Walpole*, op. cit., vol. VIII (1904).
[9] Walpole to Mann, 4 August 1774, ibid., vol. ix (1907).

in a chaise, they arrived at Genoa, where they embarked uncomfortably in a felucca for Antibes, were pursued by pirates, but arrived safely and continued by land to Paris. Thence Walpole travelled alone to London, having been away almost two and a half years.

He had been happier in Florence than ever before, but after his return to England he never went back, though he continued to correspond with Mann over the next forty-five years. The rebuilding of his 'little Gothic castle' Strawberry Hill became Walpole's chief occupation after 1750. From there he replied, almost daily, to the daily letters from Horace Mann; but they had a pact between them, that every letter had to be returned to its sender—for, of course, the letters were going to be useful to them when they came to write their autobiographies, as they never doubted they one day would. Walpole's letters are of greater literary value than Mann's, which were often tedious, but the latter's are a unique record, which kept his younger friend in touch with all the gossip and political events in Italy.

During Horace Walpole's stay in Florence, Mann had seemed to be on the best of terms with the Florentines, but with the fall from power of Sir Robert Walpole. his sponsor, in 1742, he was aware of a slight cooling-off on the part of local society; and unfounded rumours were circulated about him by Walpole's unpleasant sister-in-law. Mann was thereafter noticeably more critical of the Florentines, in whom he was somewhat disappointed, having perhaps made too many swans out of geese.

Walpole had not been pleased by the Florentines who descended on him in England, claiming a return of hospitality, and Mann complained that he, for his part, was even expected to have things brought in from England, such as orange-flower water, then in great demand, for the Florentines. But the social life continued to be diverting. In the summer he gave his usual assemblies in the garden, though he dared not announce that there would be music, otherwise all the world would arrive. And at the opera he could receive in his box as if he were at home, and need only go a few steps from the box to make visits, or else he could concentrate on the music.

Mann did have one close friend among the Florentines: Cocchi, the well-known anglophile physician. Having studied with the foremost medical authorities in London and in Holland in 1726-8, he applied their teachings when he became Professor of Surgery at the Hospital of Santa Maria Nuova and head of various local committees charged with drawing up medical and hygienic regulations. A man of wide interests and an excellent linguist, speaking English without an accent, Cocchi filled his diary with passages in Hebrew and Arabic, and was able to decipher a ninth-century Byzantine manuscript on the works of the early Greek surgeons. He was also a literary critic, and discovered and published the *Autobiography* of Benvenuto Cellini. Wilton's powerful bust of him, in the Victoria and Albert Museum,[10] is undraped, in the classical style—though actually the doctor had undisciplined long hair and wore his shirts untidily unbuttoned, in the later Byronic mode.

Horace Mann continued throughout his career to exert himself on behalf of the British in Tuscany. At the end of January 1742, soon after Walpole's return to England, there was a severe earthquake at Leghorn and minor tremors were felt afterwards which terrified the population. 'All the houses, they say, have suffered extremely, particularly the Jews' quarter. Part of a church fell in, and some people have been killed. All the inhabitants fled out of the town, and everything was in horrid confusion,' Mann reported to his young friend. The barracks had been damaged and tents were required to house the troops. Although Goldworthy, the British Consul at Leghorn, had been intriguing to supplant Mann at Florence, Mann with characteristic kindness wrote immediately to the Consul's wife to offer her and her family shelter. 'Common humanity,' he told Walpole, 'engages me to press her to come from that horrid place, and to forget everything they have said and done against me. I suppose my letter will find them on board some ship in the Mole, as nobody lives in their houses.'

On 3 February he wrote of the damage being at present unmeasured because people dared not return to their homes from fear of another earthquake. Many families fled to Pisa and Lucca

[10] 'One of [Wilton's] most distinguished works . . . without parallel in its day in Europe', says Margaret Whinney, *English Sculptors 1720–1830* (HMSO, 1971).

with only the clothes they were wearing. The English had taken refuge on the ships in the harbour and had taken books and money there. Those who had to remain in the town spent their days and nights in the main square, sleeping in coaches or on chairs until tents could be erected.

Mrs Goldworthy took advantage of Mann's offer of hospitality a day earlier than he had expected, bringing three children, two maids, and a man servant. Mann sympathized with her sad story but he foresaw difficulties with her. She filled his entire house, with the exception of two rooms downstairs to which he retired, and she stayed on long after the danger in Leghorn was past. The lady irritated Mann beyond words by assuring her children that if they prayed for Jesus to be in the room He would touch their baby sister and she would cut her teeth!

In the later 1740s Mann's letters to Walpole anxiously follow the course of the Jacobite rising set off when the Young Pretender, Bonnie Prince Charlie, gave Mann's spies the slip and left Italy for Scotland in 1745. In January 1746, owing to the lack of post, Mann was fearful that the rising had succeeded and that the Jacobites were 'masters of London'. But such reports, he conceded, usually originated in France and were echoed from Rome. It was 31 May 1746, however, before Mann had final news of the defeat of Charles Edward. The English victory at Culloden was welcomed, of course, but he wrote of the trial of the Jacobite lords with his natural kindliness: 'if the King shows mercy, I shall be glad. . . .'

Mann had been almost overwhelmed by his failure to keep track of Charles Edward Stuart immediately before the 1745 rebellion, and over the next decades he assiduously followed the Prince's every movement. When Walpole wrote in 1762 that the birth of a Prince of Wales in London assured the Hanoverian succession, Sir Horace replied that the Old Pretender's life was drawing to a close, whilst 'his devout son [Cardinal York] contents himself with praying for him. The other [Prince Charles Edward] will probably get drunk to drown his sorrow.' When James Edward, acknowledged as James III, died in Rome at the beginning of 1766, and Charles Edward—with the support of the French Ambassador—claimed his father's titles, Mann lobbied the Pope and afterwards claimed credit for Clement XIII's refusal finally to acknowledge the Young Pretender's rights.

When, some years later, after his marriage to Louise of Stolberg, Charles Edward decided to live in Florence, Sir Horace was aghast: this meant trouble for him. And trouble there certainly was, for in 1776, while staying in a palazzo lent to him by Prince Corsini, Charles (known as the Count of Albany) sought to buy the Palazzo Guadagni.[11] The proprietor was somewhat reluctant to sell, having no doubt heard that the Grand Duke of Tuscany, Peter Leopold, was of the same mind as Horace Mann regarding the descent upon Florence of the Bonnie (but drunken) Prince Charlie. In the meantime the wealthy Earl Cowper, whose wife was pregnant and who wanted to take a house in the city for her confinement, had proposed to the proprietor that he should rent the Palazzo Guadagni for a few months. As Mann wrote to Walpole:

> This displeased the Comte Albanie and the dispute was carried to the publick Tribunal, which decided in the Comte's favour. This displeased the Great [Grand] Duke, who favoured the Cowpers. In short, the whole town took part in it, but I dissuaded my Lord from making an appeal to another court, so that the Albanies now reside in it; though the contract heightened the price considerably. What the Comte complained of most was, that he should meet with so rebellious an opposition from one of his own subjects.

George Nassau Clavering, third Earl Cowper, who had given up his seat in Parliament in order to remain in Florence, had married Miss Anne Gore in 1775, and it was said that he owed his position at the Tuscan court to her attraction for the Grand Duke. However, Cowper and the Grand Duke also shared an interest in music and in science. Peter Leopold was a great patron of science, financing a laboratory and a museum as well as increasing the number of science chairs at the University of Pisa; Cowper also befriended the scientists of the day, had his own laboratory in the Via Ghibellina, and took an active part in scientific and learned societies.

[11] See chapter IV; p. 52.

Mann, who had no interest in science, was undoubtedly jealous of Cowper's closeness to the Grand Duke; at the same time, he did not hesitate to make use of him politically. In 1779, when both France and Spain were at war with England, supplies were reaching the British garrisons at Gibraltar and Minorca illegally, at Mann's instigation, through the neutral port of Leghorn, which must have embarrassed the Tuscan government. The British Government was preparing to launch a proposal for a separate peace with Spain, and Mann was instructed to drop a hint to the Grand Duke that he might be able to help with this. Mann had to explain that an audience with the Grand Duke was granted to foreign diplomats only by special request; 'I therefore,' he wrote to the Earl of Hillsborough, 'had recourse as usual, to Lord Cowper. . . . His Lordship lives in the utmost familiarity with His Royal Highness.' And it was to Cowper that Peter Leopold passed on the decision of himself and his brother the Emperor, that it was not possible to help.

Matters of protocol, and relations with the Court, had played an increasingly important part in Sir Horace Mann's life since 1765, the year in which he at last received the title of Envoy from His Britannic Majesty to the Grand Duke of Tuscany. With the title, forwarded through Sir John Dick, British Consul at Genoa, came the insignia of the Order of the Bath. Mann wrote off to share his joy with Walpole:

> The Italians expect a great deal on this occasion, and it has so happened that the extraordinary number and great rank of the English here at present, many of whom have stayed on purpose, will make my cortege or procession to Court that morning most brilliant. . . . The Duke of Devonshire will condescend to accompany me thither; Earl Cowper, Earl Tylney, Lord Algernon Percy, Lord Fortrose, Sir Watkin W. Wynne, Sir George Turner, and at least thirty more English Gentlmen all as fine as the richest Peers.

He gave a ball the following evening and on the next day, Sunday, Lord Tylney gave a grand dinner, 'the most magnificent I ever saw', as his guest of honour described it. Tylney, a member of the Royal Society who dabbled in the study of volcanoes, had a house near the Chiesa del Carmine which amazed the Italians with its coloured wallpapers.

In the following year, the Grand Duke Peter Leopold paid his first state visit to Leghorn, prompting many entertainments and formalities which Mann attended:

> The English merchants and their dependants gave us a *Calcio*—a fine football in Gala, performed in the Great Square; fifty on a side, with their officers very richly dressed, at the cost of above a thousand pounds. One uniform was rose-coloured satin; the other, blue. The first appearance, and their march, made the prettiest show imaginable; but the sequel did not answer—both from the inexperience of the players, and an absolute prohibition to give serious blows with their fists, without which the game must be languid.

However, the match was repeated two days later more violently, to the general satisfaction of the spectators.

Mann was constantly being asked to perform small services for the ducal rulers. When the Grand Duchess decided to learn English seriously, Mann recommended an English Carmelite friar, Edward Barker, who had come to his notice when Barker asked permission to dedicate an English–Italian grammar to him. She also asked His Britannic Majesty's Envoy to procure two English King Charles spaniels for her. 'Could you get them of the very smallest size and of particular beauty among the Royal Descendants?' wrote Sir Horace, asking Walpole's help on this delicate matter.

As Peter Leopold was next in line to the throne of the Austrian Empire, Vienna was very much deferred to at the Court of Florence; the Grand Duke and Duchess could not even attend a ball without the Emperor's permission, lest it have diplomatic repercussions. When the brother of Queen Charlotte of England visited Florence from Mecklenburg, Mann had to introduce him in great state to the Court. He was much gratified when they were invited to dine with the Grand Duke at one of his country houses, at Poggio, which was considered more of an honour than dining at the Pitti Palace in Florence.

When Lord and Lady Holland were in Florence in 1767,

Mann reported that he 'omitted nothing which her high birth and their situation could suggest to tickle Austrian ears'; and the Court gave permission that Lord Holland should be carried in a sedan chair into 'the most sacred part of the Palace' where only 'the *Dame dell'Accesso* can approach'. But Mann's tact and diplomacy were not always so successful; to his chagrin, some English visitors were invited to dine at Court and others not. Walpole sometimes laughed at his friend's worries over his 'playing court'; 'An English Member of Parliament is part of the Legislature, and what is a Tuscan nobleman part of? Has not that haughty Empress Queen [Maria Theresa] been our pensioner?'

Meanwhile Mann himself continued to dispense hospitality and succour to British visitors. In 1764 William Hamilton, British envoy at Naples, and his (first) wife, 'cast into Leghorn some days ago by a storm', whilst waiting for a favourable wind came to Florence to call on Mann. But there, Sir Horace told Walpole, 'The poor, good sickly lady was seized with a fit of the asthma, as she got out of the coach, at my door, and could with difficulty get to her appartment. . . . Did not your ears tingle? For we talked of nothing else but of you and your Château at Strawberry?'

Asthma seems to have been a popular malady, for one of George III's brothers, the Duke of Gloucester (who had married a niece of Sir Robert Walpole), was stricken with it while travelling in Italy in 1771, and when partially recovered, moved into Mann's house in Via Santo Spirito to convalesce. The Duke and his attendants treated the place as an inn, and behaved outrageously to Mann. The Duke, then thirty-two, had been so ill it was thought he would not live long, but apparently he had so many different doctors—two of them sent out from England by the King—that as each prescribed different medicines and threw away those of his predecessor, the patient recovered from the lack of medicines, to live another thirty years!

Though England was at war with France, all this time George III was buying enormous quantities of Italian works of art; Mann believed no ship left Italy without something on board destined for the King's collection. Mann's own private means were not great and it is clear that his salary in Florence would not have enabled him to fulfil his duties and to provide entertainment for so many visitors, had he not made himself into an art dealer; in the process he became something of a collector himself. At this period there were no famous artists in Florence for whom he could have acted as agent in the way that Joseph Smith did in Venice (selling many items to George III); but he did form a lifelong friendship with Thomas Patch, who came to live just across the street from him, supplied Horace Walpole with some of Patch's work, and arranged for Patch to dedicate to Walpole a volume of Fra Bartolommeo's engravings. He also helped gain permission for visiting artists to copy pictures in the Florentine galleries, and sometimes obtained copies for clients of pictures in the great private collections, for which he received a commission and often a personal gift for his trouble.

In 1779 the painting by Zoffany of the Tribuna, the great octagonal salon in the Uffizi, caused a stir in Florence, and in Sir Horace Mann. The artist, on a commission from Queen Charlotte, had decided to include in the huge canvas the chief figures of Florence. There was no doubt much soul-searching over the selection of those figures and a painful anxiety as Florentines waited for the invitation to pose for the artist. Mann may or may not have been involved in the choice of subjects; but, being one of the chosen, he shows an endearing ability to laugh at himself:

> As to the question you [Walpole] make me of my own personage, I can only say that everybody thought it like me, but I suppose Zoffany took pains to lessen my pot-belly and the clumsiness of my figure, and to make me stand in a posture which I never kept to. . . .

Walpole replied that he could not find the Mann he knew in the picture: 'My dear sir, how you have left me in the lurch! You have grown fat, jolly, young, while I am become the skeleton of Methuselah . . .',[12] and went on sarcastically:

[12] One of Walpole's neighbours at Twickenham has brought the master of Strawberry Hill most vividly to life at this time: '. . . he always entered a room in that style of affected delicacy, which fashion had then made almost natural; . . . knees bent and feet on tiptoe, as if afraid of a wet floor.' (Lactitia-Matilda Hawkins, *Anecdotes, Biographical Sketches and Memoirs* (1822–4), vol. I.)

I do allow Earl Cowper a place in the Tribune; an Englishman who has never seen his earldom, who takes root and bears fruit in Florence, and is proud of a pinchbeck principality in a third country, is as great a curiosity as any in the Tuscan collection.

Mann, alas, had not grown jolly and young, as Walpole teased, and his last years were made uneasy by the fact that the powerful Earl Cowper wanted to supplant him as Minister. He now belonged to Florence; unwell and failing in his powers, it was too late for him to return to England. Although he remained convinced that his own country was superior in every respect to Italy, in Florence he was treated with an affection and respect which he feared he would not find at home. He lacked Cowper's ability to speak several languages and to indulge a vast range of interests, and his willingness, and the power of his wealth, to encourage talent in these fields. Yet Mann's integrity and kindness, and his interest in the day-to-day gossip of the Florentines and the Anglo-Florentines made him in Italian eyes the epitome of the Englishman of his time.

In 1780 Mann's spirits were raised by Admiral Rodney's victory over the Spanish fleet; when he reported the news to the Grand Duke, the latter clearly showed his sympathies with Britain. Many ships now arrived at Leghorn and Civitavecchia, and the Pope, as Mann wrote to Walpole, was delighted to have shipping opened in the Mediterranean, so that his flock could have fish for Lent.

In 1781 Horace Walpole's wild sister-in-law, now the Countess of Orford, died at Pisa and was buried according to her wish, like so many other Anglo-Tuscans, in the English cemetery at Leghorn. She had not even returned to England to see her son during his last illness, but according to a will made eight years earlier, had left everything to her Italian friend Mozzi. Sir Horace assured Walpole that Mozzi was no fortune-hunter, a member of one of the oldest Italian families, he was not without money himself. The lady, gossiped Mann, had chosen him for his looks when he was in his prime, and he wanted it to be thought that she chose him for his learning! Mozzi's own family had disapproved of his friendship with Lady Orford, as it prevented him from marrying and having an heir—an important matter since he was the last male in the family, and 'You know,' Sir Horace went on, 'that Italians consider the extinction of their name of the first importance and misfortune.'

Mann carried on his duties faithfully to the last. In 1784 the friend of Dr Johnson, Mrs Piozzi, visited him; he was 'sick and old',[13] she said, but continued to hold his weekly *conversazione* on Saturday evening. Though he had through the years passed on to Walpole so many details of the life and people of Florence, he had had few Italian intimates except Dr Cocchi. It was thirty years since the Earl of Cork had described him as living in the 'friendship, skill and care' of Dr Cocchi, adding: 'Could I live with these two gentlemen only, and converse with few or none others, I should scarce desire to return to England for many years.'[14]

Significant of the affection and respect in which Sir Horace Mann was held by the Tuscan people, on his death in November 1786 the memorial service in Leghorn, preached by Robert Hall, was translated into Italian and published with a *Notte* by Ciarametti. As he had wished, his body was taken back to England and buried at Linton, his family home.

[13] Hester Lynch Piozzi, *Autobiography* (1861).
[14] John Nichols *Literary Anecdotes of the Eighteenth Century*, vol. I (1782).

VI

Three Eighteenth-Century Painters and their Patrons: Patch, Zoffany and Angelica Kauffmann

I

OF three English painters of the eighteenth century—Thomas Patch, Johann Zoffany and Angelica Kauffmann—who owed much to the inspiration acquired during lengthy sojourns in Florence, only the first was actually born and bred in England. Though Thomas Patch made his fame and his fortune in Florence and never went home again, he came from Exeter, where he was born in 1725 into a family of surgeons which was of some importance in the county. Thomas's father had been surgeon to the Old Pretender, James Edward Stuart, at the Palace of St-Germain; in spite of that, he later became chief surgeon at the hospital in Hanoverian Exeter. Thomas's brother James, also a surgeon, had a house whose grounds became one of the chief parks of the city. Thomas too was expected to enter the medical profession, but his aptitude for drawing led him to rebel. He was sent to London to live with and study under a learned physician, Dr Mead; but Mead, a cultured gentleman, also had antiquarian interests, and in his house Patch met people who could ease his way to becoming an artist.

In his early twenties he travelled to Italy on foot, in the company of Richard Dalton (afterwards librarian to George III), and studied at the French Academy in Rome from 1749 to 1755. Claude-Joseph Vernet, the French artist, in 1750 took Patch into his studio in Rome, where he stayed for three years, until Vernet left the city. Although nothing has survived of Patch's Roman work, the harbour and river scenes he painted later in Florence show the influence of Vernet (whom Patch thought a better artist than Claude); indeed his early work was so close to that of his master that a number of paintings formerly attributed to Vernet have now been shown to be by Patch.

In 1749 Joshua Reynolds came to Rome, where he studied for two years, and at one time he and Patch lived in the same house; Patch wrote with obvious pleasure to his family of being in lodgings with Reynolds and Vernet, where he was able to live on a guinea a week. Reynolds did a set of caricatures of the chief members of the English colony in Rome, in the most important of which, a parody of Raphael's *School of Athens,* Patch appears. Patch himself does not seem to have taken up caricature at this time.

Lord Charlemont, friend and patron of the arts, had a group of artists working for him in Rome at the time who referred to themselves as an Academy, though they had, of course, no such status. When Charlemont went off to the Middle East, taking Patch's friend Richard Dalton with him, he left Patch with a commission to do pictures of the countryside around Rome, and ordered especially views of Tivoli. Cardinal Albani, writing in October 1751 to Sir Horace Mann, the British envoy in Florence, noted that Patch had been in Tivoli working for his patron during the three summer months of 1750 and again in 1751.[1]

However, Patch, as a Protestant, seems to have gone out of his way to annoy the Vatican authorities; the art dealer and agent, John Parker, and others reported that he was rash in the provocative way he declared his anti-Catholic views. Whilst working at Tivoli he was abruptly ordered by the Bishop of Tivoli to leave the diocese. Horace Mann, inquiring of Cardinal Albani as to the cause of this order, pointed out that even a denounced heretic was usually allowed eight days to arrange his departure from a Catholic state. But the Bishop of Tivoli, when questioned directly as to why Patch was to be sent away, was evasive, hinting at some unmentionable crime, and Parker later wrote to Lord Charlemont that there had been a scandal about

---

[1] MS letter, Austrian State Archives.

Patch's 'girl of Tivoli'.[2] But Parker, the Earl's agent in Rome, may simply have been jealous of Patch's success with His Lordship. In any event, doubtless because Pope Benedict XIV was a close friend of Lord Charlemont, the scandal seems to have been hushed up, and Patch was allowed to remain in Rome. Charlemont continued his patronage, and large sums were paid for the packing and dispatching of Patch's pictures to Charlemont's estate in Ireland.

A few months later, however, a further and heavier blow fell. Patch was ordered by the Vatican to leave the Papal States within twenty-four hours, and this time it appeared there was no appeal: he had to pack up and go. He was undoubtedly a quarrelsome person and may not have been altogether truthful when in a letter to his patron attempting to vindicate his conduct, he maintained he had not had any dispute, or even any talk of religion, for the past year. But the agent Parker, from all accounts a bitter, unpleasant character, continued to spread scandal about him, writing in 1756 to Lord Charlemont that Patch had been banished, 'some say', for 'B—y, others [for] giving a potion to a Nun to make her miscarry . . .'[3]

Patch went from Rome to Florence, where he arrived with letters of recommendation to the Governor, Count Richecourt, from Monsignor Piccolomini, to Horace Mann, Lord Huntingdon and others of the English set. Sir William Stanhope had come to his rescue by purchasing two landscapes, and he still had a portion of the hundred pounds recently paid him by Sir William Lowther, so he wasn't starving. And new commissions came his way; he was soon completing 'a bridge painting for Lord Huntingdon'.[4] Sixteen years later, as Horace Mann mentioned in one of his gossipy letters to Horace Walpole, the artist was still in Florence.

Indeed, the British envoy had become Patch's firm ally. The painter by then had a house on the opposite side of Via Santo Spirito from the Casa Manetti where Mann lived, and there was never a day that he was not at his friend's house. Through Mann

---

[2] His. MSS Commission, Twelfth Report, Appendix Part X. MSS & Corres. of James 1st Earl of Charlemont (1891), p. 223.

[3] MS letter of 26 Feb. 1756, in possession of the Royal Irish Academy.

[4] Charlemont Papers, loc. cit., p. 225.

he met many of the British living in or passing through Florence. The latter were often very happy to find a talented painter who could produce a view of the Arno or one of its bridges which they could buy for a few golden guineas and take home as a souvenir of their tour. Patch worked consistently on such paintings. The view he most often chose was of the Ponte di Santa Trinitá from the north side of the Arno. The paintings were usually copied from the engravings of Patch's friend Giuseppe Zocchi; he varied the position of the boats on the river and the groups of people on either bank, but never omitted the little coach and galloping horses crossing the bridge which were to be seen in Zocchi's engravings. (Two of these delightful pictures can be seen in Florence today, one large one in the office of the Director of the Uffizi Gallery, and a second, slightly smaller and having fewer boats, in the fascinating museum *Firenze Com'era* (Florence as it was).) Patch also made numerous paintings of the Piazza della Signoria from the north side, varying the figures, and sometimes adding soldiers drilling, or a Punch and Judy show. Several of his paintings are in the Royal Albert Memorial Museum of Exeter.

When Patch had been working in this vein for some years, Horace Mann suggested that his friend Walpole should accept two of Patch's views of Florence for his 'little Gothic box' at Strawberry Hill, and these reached him in time for Christmas 1771.[5] Walpole remarked that the views were 'a little Hard', hoping that Patch would accept this as constructive criticism. It seems that, after a visit to Venice in 1760, Patch had begun to use the colder tone of Canaletto instead of the more luminous effect of Vernet. (Some of his work has even been ascribed to Canaletto in the salerooms.[6]) He did not, however, cease to paint imaginary harbour scenes in the Vernet manner for the tourists; Mann had four of these in the large reception room of Casa Manetti, which must have given pleasure to the owner and acted as an advertisement for the artist.

For all his success as a landscape artist, Patch today is best

[5] Mann to Walpole, 22 February 1771; Walpole to Mann, 24 March and 28 December 1771, *Letters of Horace Walpole*, ed. Paget Toynbee, vol. VIII (1904).
[6] F. J. B. Watson, 'Life of Thomas Patch' *Walpole Society Papers* vol., XXVIII (1939-40).

Charles Edward Stuart when he was living in Florence, painted by H. D. Hamilton.

Maria Clementina Sobieska in about 1719, painted by an unidentified artist.

Top left The royal arms of England on a wall of the Palazzo Guadagni, which is now the school of architecture of the University of Florence. *Top right* Canova's monument to the Stuarts in St Peter's, Rome. It is said that on a recent visit to Rome Queen Elizabeth II, following an initiative of the Queen Mother, showed an interest in improving the tombs of the Stuarts in the crypt of St Peter's. *Left* The Countess of Albany's monument in Santa Croce, Florence.

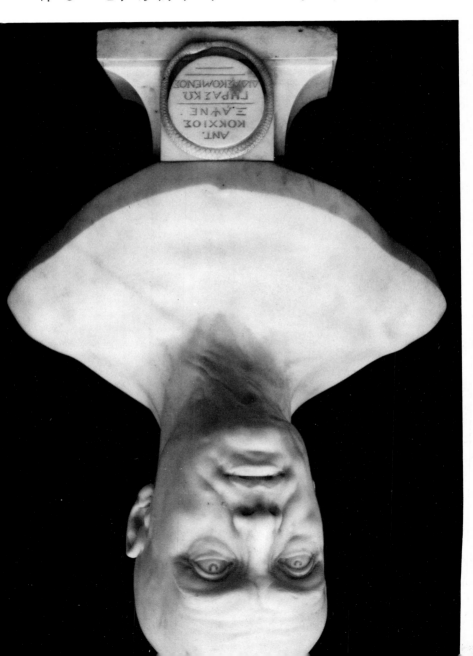

A bust by J. Wilton of Sir Horace Mann's anglophile friend, Doctor Cocchi.

A detail from Zoffany's 'The Tribuna'. Zoffany himself is showing Titian's
'Venus' to Sir Horace Mann and Thomas Patch. Mann is wearing the insignia
of the Order of the Garter; Patch is just behind him, looking over Zoffany's
shoulder.

known for his flair for caricature. In Venice in 1760 he was with an English party which included Lord Gray (later Earl Stamford), Sir Henry Mainwaring and the Revd Jonathan Lipyeatt, depicted by Patch as *The Punch Party*. His satirical drawings and paintings made an immediate impression, and within a few years he was in constant demand for this type of work. He did it without cruelty and, as Mann relates, 'He was always so prudent as never to caricature anybody without his consent and a full liberty to exert his talents.'[7] As Patch caricatured himself, and at least as savagely as he did others, among the groups he depicted, no one could complain. His portrayals were not hostile to their subjects, but were mere humorous comments, achieved by the exaggeration of some prominent characteristic, such as the heavy under-jaw of the rich Lord Cowper, then the social arbiter of Florence.

In 1764 the Duke of York arrived in the city and ordered a painting from Patch. The picture seems to have vanished, but fortunately Horace Mann wrote a full account of it to Walpole. Apparently the Duke was painted leaving Mann's house, surrounded by all the well-known figures of the British colony.

About 1765 Patch also started engraving. Some of his quick sketches may have been engraved directly on to wood or copper, but the most important ones were based on drawings which he meticulously reworked. He had been greatly impressed by the famous Masaccio frescoes in the Brancacci Chapel of the church of the Carmine, not two hundred yards from where he lived, and he made careful and precise drawings of them which he etched on copper. The twenty-six plates were published in 1770 as *The Life of the Celebrated Painter, Masaccio*, with a dedication to Sir Horace Mann. In his brief biography of the painter, Patch included a discussion of fresco painting which shows a profound professional understanding. At this time the Italian Primitives, as we call the early pre-Renaissance painters, were not much valued (they were waiting for Ruskin's appraisal); Patch was perhaps the first artist of his time to arrive at a true appreciation of them. He also made a series of wood engravings from the Giotto

---

[7] Mann to Walpole, February 1771, in Dr J. Doran, *'Mann' and Manners at the Court of Florence, 1740–1786* (1876), vol. II.

frescoes of the life of John the Baptist in the Manetti Chapel of the Carmine, writing in the introduction to the published engravings, 'After all I think I am the first that has ever given prints after this Author to the Public . . .'[8] The precision of his copying was a great blessing for posterity, for in January 1771 a great fire in the church of the Carmine damaged every Masaccio. It was from Patch's drawings of the frescoes that artists worked to accomplish the excellent restoration. The Giottos were completely ruined in the same fire and our appreciation of them today derives mainly from Patch's copies.

Patch sent copies of the volume of Masaccio engravings to England, where they were sold at a high price by Patch's brother, the surgeon James. Mann sent a presentation copy to Horace Walpole, who responded with enthusiasm: 'I am transported with them, I did not remember these works. Oh! if there are more make your Patch give us all. I cannot be content under all.'[9] He would show them to Sir Joshua Reynolds, he said, and suggested Patch should make a similar set from Fra Bartolommeo, 'another parent of Raphael, whose ideas, I thought, even greater.' A volume of these was published towards the end of 1772, and Patch declared he intended to 'publish as many works of this celebrated Author as are to be found in Tuscany', but the five-volume project was abandoned. When he was brought the Fra Bartolommeo volume by James Patch, together with a volume of the engravings after Giotto, Walpole criticised them rather unkindly, but later he took back his criticism and declared he was ready 'to subscribe for anything of Mr Patch's'. Indeed, Walpole was so impressed by the precision of Patch's engravings that he asked Mann if the artist could do 'a drawing of yourself, of your whole person exactly as you are . . .'[10] But such a drawing has never been traced—if, indeed, it was ever executed.

Patch's greatest contribution to art history was the publication of an account of the construction of Ghiberti's doors to the Baptistry in Florence. Basing his work on a contemporary MS then in the possession of the Arte de' Fabricanti (it has since dis-

---

[8] *The Life of Giotto* (1772), quoted in catalogue of Exhibition of British Art, 1934.
[9] Walpole to Mann, 20 January 1771, *Letters*, op. cit. vol. VIII.
[10] Walpole to Mann, 20 January 1771, ibid.

appeared), with the help of Ferdinando Gregori he illustrated the book with twenty-four engravings of details the same size as the original, based on 'Casts recently moulded on the Original Gates'. The book, *The Gates of the Baptistry of St John in Florence* (1774) is very rare indeed; the British Library has no copy, and the Victoria and Albert Museum only an imperfect one.

Johann Zoffany admired Patch and gave him one of the much sought-after places in his paintings of the Tribuna;[11] he is shown beside Titian's *Venus of Urbino*, turning to talk to Sir Horace Mann and pointing to the sculptures behind. But Patch and Zoffany later had a dispute over money. Two pictures commissioned from Patch by a M. Durad of Geneva were handed over to Zoffany, to be delivered by him in Switzerland—presumably on his way home to England; he was then to collect Patch's fee. But when it was learned that Zoffany was about to leave Florence without settling this account, Patch applied to the *commendatore* of the *quartiere* of Santo Spirito to prevent his fellow painter's departure until payment had been made.[12]

Patch did at times himself consider returning to England, but maintained that all his family, except his father, had forgotten him; and as long as his friend Horace Mann lived near by he had no real wish to go back to his native land. Patch's brother James had married a widow, Mrs Caulet, and in November 1778 her son, Gideon Caulet, arrived to visit his step-uncle. He was greeted at Leghorn by a rumour that Thomas Patch had died, but on reaching Florence he found the artist in much better health than he expected, and he was immediately taken to Mann's for dinner.

Patch, as he told Caulet, had been a victim of the theft of some of his important work. For seven years he had studied physiognomy, as set out in the treatise by Lavater, which was then in fashion, in order to facilitate his drawing of caricatures. From this study, he said, 'he had found out ye Means of knowing at Sight what a Man's profession was, in what county he was born, and in what situation of that county—what his religion was and to what sect of that religion he belonged—what his situation in

[11] See below, p. 89ff.
[12] Arch. di Stato Firenze, Al Sigr. Comm. del Quartiere S. Spirito, li 25 Marzo 1778, no. 353.

Life was, respecting Marriage etc.' Patch had produced a work which included 'the Means by which a Painter might draw ye likeness of any Person tho he had never seen him and many other singular mentions which no Person I believe ever thought of.' He engraved six copper plates to illustrate the book, and in a subsequent group caricature (which became the property of the Duchess of Roxburghe) portrayed himself clasping the three MS volumes of his work under his arm and holding up one of the copper plates.

The work caused much interest in Florence, and especially in 'a French Duke', who made off with the volumes when he returned to France. Pursued to Marseilles, where he was asked to return the work he had 'borrowed', the nobleman in panic threw the whole thing into the fire. Thus, remarked Gideon Caulet, 'we are for ever deprived of a set of most Curious observations and reflections.' Not even Patch's notes survived, 'as to avoid confusion they were burnt.' All the same, wrote Caulet, who was justifiably proud of his uncle, 'his works in Florence are sufficient to entitle him to Immortality and to rank his name amongst the first painters of Italy.'[13]

But the loss of his volumes on physiognomy seems to have robbed Patch of the will to work, and he painted very little from this time until his death four years after his nephew's departure for England. On 29 April 1782, Patch suffered an attack of apoplexy whilst in Horace Mann's house. He rushed across the road to his own house where he flung himself on the bed; when Mann arrived he was unable to speak, and he died next morning.[14] He is said to have been buried in England, but the present Soperintendente of the Uffizi Gallery maintains that he was buried in the Covent of the Carmine. If he was, his grave is unmarked.

One of Patch's paintings of Florence is in the Queen's collection, and two of his views of the Arno are at Hampton Court. A few of his drawings are in the Print Room of the British Museum.

---

[13] Watson, op. cit.
[14] Mann to Walpole, 30 April 1782, in Doran, op. cit., vol. II.

86

2

It was soon after Patch's volume of Masaccio engravings was published that Johann Zoffany arrived on the art scene in Florence. The erstwhile German painter's self-portrait, given by him in 1778 to the Grand Duke of Tuscany for his collection in the Uffizi, has a most arresting quality. He is smiling, yet there is a haunting sadness in the eyes. The luxuriously furred coat suggests material wealth, but is belied by the hourglass and the skull which he is holding; the *écorché* figure above in the background, and the motto on the book next to it, *Ars longa vita brevis*, sound a melancholy note.

Zoffany, who caused more talk in Florence than any other painter from England, had been born in Germany in 1733 and brought up at the small court of the Prince of Thurn und Taxis. After a period of study in Rome, he was given employment at the Electoral Court of Trier. He then went to England, where David Garrick commissioned him to paint episodes from his theatre productions, which set him firmly on the road to success. From 1762 he exhibited paintings of actors in their roles, and particularly of Garrick himself, painted with meticulous accuracy of gesture. (Many of his paintings relating to the theatre have been lovingly preserved in the Garrick Club in London.) His portrait of Garrick as the Alchymist, exhibited at the Royal Academy in 1769, was bought by Sir Joshua Reynolds himself; he also exhibited a portrait of the King, George III, by whom he had been nominated as a Royal Academician.

Surprisingly one discovers that in 1772, when he was thirty-nine, Zoffany was ready to sail with Captain Cook on his second voyage of exploration in the Southern Hemisphere; owing to some disagreement the arrangement was cancelled. Much later he painted the scene of *The Death of Captain Cook* which is now in the National Maritime Museum, Greenwich. But in 1772, instead of voyaging to the South Seas, the painter set out for Italy.

By then he had a royal patron, Queen Charlotte (also a German), who paid for his journey to Florence, and provided him with introductions to influential persons there. Of course he met

Horace Mann, His Majesty's Envoy in the Tuscan capital, and Mann used his influence on his behalf with the Grand Duke Leopold, who took a liking to Zoffany and his work. But, significantly, it was to George Nassau, 3rd Earl Cowper, the most important figure in the Florentine English colony, that Zoffany brought an introduction from Queen Charlotte. The letter, written by Lady Spencer at Her Majesty's behest in June 1772, ran:

> I have the Queen's commands to recommend Zoffani, a painter and a very ingenious man, to your Lordship's protection. Her Majesty sends him to Florence and wishes to have him admitted into the Great Duke's Gallery [i.e., the Uffizi] this I have no doubt will be a sufficient Motive for your Lordship's gaining him every advantage in your power but I cannot in justice to the Man help adding that he has uncommon Merit and has distinguish'd himself very much in the stile of Portrait Painting.[15]

The letter resulted in several commissions from Lord Cowper. Zoffany painted his Lordship standing, wearing what was apparently Tuscan court dress. In 1774 he painted Lord Cowper's fiancée, *Miss Anne Gore as a Savoyarde,* and the following year a charming group, *Lord Cowper and the Gore Family*, on an outdoor terrace against a Tuscan background. Mr Gore is playing the violoncello, accompanied at the piano by his daughter Emily; Lord Cowper stands behind him and his future wife Anne to the right at the front of the picture. Typical eighteenth-century German that he was, Zoffany portrayed musical instruments most lovingly and correctly, and he was superb at the conversation piece which was fashionable in Hanoverian England.

The painter apparently found difficulty in learning English; throughout his life he remained more fluent in German, and later on in Italian, than in English, which he spoke with a strong German accent. His private life had not been easy. He had married in Germany and made use of his wife's dowry to settle in England, but he appears not to have treated his wife well; she returned home and died not long afterwards. Before leaving

---

[15] Panshanger MSS in the Hertfordshire County Record Office, quoted in Oliver Millar, *Zoffany and his Tribuna* (1967).

for Italy in 1772, he dallied with a young girl who became pregnant and who hid herself on the boat on which he was to sail. He took her with him to Italy and married her. A Mrs Papendick, friend of his second wife in later days, wrote:

Dear Mrs Zoffany . . . was a perfect beauty, good-natured, kind and very charitable. She was not of equal rank with her husband, and when she married him [at] fourteen years of age having had no education, her mind was not formed. During the seven years they spent in Italy, however, she did receive some instruction, and spoke the language perfectly. Their eldest child was a boy, who died from an accident at sixteen months old. The calamity nearly lost poor Zoffany his life; indeed he never thoroughly overcame it.[16]

Judging by the portrait of her, which he painted on their return to England, one can easily believe that Zoffany's young wife had acquired polished manners, and was so charming and generous that she was accepted not only by the Anglo-Florentines, but by the Grand Duke's household. It was while her first son was in the care of the grand-ducal head nurse that the fatal accident to the child occurred. Two daughters were later born to the Zoffanys in Italy, and two more in England, but the painter could not be comforted for the loss of his son. It was at this time, perhaps fortunately, that he turned to the immense task of the *Tribuna*, for which he had received a royal commission, and which he worked on intermittently from 1772 to 1777.

The Uffizi Gallery, built by Buontalenti in 1585–9 for Francesco de Medici, was used at first as an office building, but was later adapted to house the works of art of the Medici collection; the Tribuna is its most famous room. Zoffany's painting was intended to show in a single work, for the benefit of King George IV and Queen Charlotte who would never be able to visit the Uffizi in person, the finest treasures of the Medici. The artist was given every facility and was allowed to remove from and to bring into the room any works of art he wished. (Seven pictures were in fact brought at his behest from the Pitti Palace.) The problems which faced him must have been daunting, for he

[16] *Court and Private Life in the Time of Queen Charlotte I* (1887).

had to reproduce, in relatively small copies, paintings by some of the greatest artists of the Renaissance as they hung round two walls of the room, with sculptures carefully placed for effect.

It was Zoffany's brilliant idea further to enliven the scene with living English visitors or residents of note, portrayed in natural groups as they examined the paintings and sculptures. Thus in the foreground on the right, admiring the *Venus of Urbino* by Titian, he placed Horace Mann, wearing the ribbon and star of the Order of the Bath, with Thomas Patch just behind him; on the left was Lord Cowper pointing to the Raphael *Madonna*, which was held up by Zoffany himself, who had purchased the painting in Florence and sold it to Cowper; and many other people were included. In 1779, when the picture had been seen in England, Mann wrote to Horace Walpole:

> I am glad that you have seen Zoffany and his Portrait of the Tribuna. . . . He told me that the King had expressly ordered my portrait to be there, which I did not believe, but did not object to it; but he made the same merit with all the young travellers then at Florence, some of whom he afterwards rubbed out. . . . If what he said is true, that the Queen sent him to Florence to do that picture, and gave him a large sum for his journey, the impropriety of crowding in so many unknown figures was still greater. But is it true that it is for the Queen's Closet, and that she is to give him three thousand pounds for it? . . . I should think too the naked Venus which is the principal figure, will not please Her Majesty so much as it did the young men to whom it was shewed. As to the question you make me of my own personage, I can only say that everybody thought it like me, but I suppose Zoffany took pains to lessen my pot-belly and the clumsiness of my figure, and to make me stand in a posture which I never kept to. . . .[17]

Walpole in his reply complained that 'The idea I always thought an absurd one. It is rendered more so by being crowded by a flock of travelling boys, and one does not know nor care whom.' However, he admitted that:

> The execution is good; most of the styles of painters happily imitated, the labour and finishing infinite; and no confusion,

[17] Doran, op. cit., vol. II.

though such a multiplicity of objects and colours. . . . though Zoffany might have been better employed. His talent is representing natural humour. I look upon him as a Dutch painter polished or civilised.[18]

Zoffany came in for a certain amount of ridicule in Florence when he styled himself 'The Queen of England's Painter in Ordinary', a title which he had not been accorded. Nevertheless, the Grand Duke presented him to the Emperor Joseph, when he came on a visit to Florence, as 'The Queen of England's Painter'. Zoffany painted portraits of the Imperial family, and the family group of *Pietro Leopoldo Grand Duke of Tuscany with his family*, against the background of the courtyard of the Pitti Palace, is charmingly intimate yet dignified. A special carriage was constructed for Zoffany to carry the painting to Vienna on its completion; there he was honoured by the Empress with the title Baron of the Holy Roman Empire. He was not without vanity, for afterwards his servants wore liveries of scarlet and gold with blue facings, the colours of the Imperial arms granted to him.

As a painter of individual portraits Zoffany was superb, depicting materials and settings with supreme care. He seemed most at home, however, in his artistic response to the Italian scene, as we see, for example, in *The Florentine Fruit Stall*, which he seems to have painted for himself and kept with him until his death. His Italian views and backgrounds are painted with obvious affection and are less conventional than his other work. Yet the *Tribuna*, his *chef d'œuvre*, was much criticized in England, and the excessive time he had taken to finish it led to a loss of the royal favour. This meant that he was no longer fashionable in London.

Disappointed by the lack of commissions after his successes in Florence, he departed for India and there painted the rich and important, both Indian and English, in their Indian settings, which he seemed to delight in. *Mr and Mrs Warren Hastings* was one of the portraits painted during his five years in India, during which time he is said to have made a fortune. He returned to England in 1798 and painted one of the most celebrated conversation pieces, of his friend Charles Townley in his library in

[18] *Letters of Horace Walpole*, op. cit., vol. IX (1904).

Park Street, among his antique marbles. Zoffany last exhibited at the Royal Academy in 1800, after which he seems to have given up painting. He died in 1810 at Strand on the Green, and was buried in Kew churchyard.

3

A contemporary of Patch and Zoffany in Italy was Angelica Kauffmann, whose name if mentioned today probably brings to mind the ceilings of the Royal Academy entrance in London, and the classical medallion-type paintings which she was commissioned to do for the Adam houses in England. The figures in these were graceful yet hardly arresting. In fact, however, Angelica was a woman of many gifts and would have been considered outstanding even today. She became an excellent portrait painter, blessed with an unusual ability to concentrate and to work extremely hard for long periods. She was fortunate also in possessing a singing voice which would have taken her far in the world of opera, had she had musical training; and she had a marked facility for languages. All this was coupled with an attractive, almost beautiful face, and a personality of great sweetness and gentleness. No wonder she was wooed and loved by some of the most talented painters of the eighteenth century.

Angelica was born in 1741 at Coire (Chur) in the Swiss canton of Grisons (Graubunden), and as a child was taught to paint by her father, Joseph Johann Kauffmann. When the family moved to Como she was invited, though only eleven, to paint the portrait of the Bishop. They then moved to Milan where the Governor, Rinaldo d'Este, Duke of Modena, was charmed by the youthful prodigy. There, however, tragedy struck, in the sudden death of Frau Kauffmann, a quiet young woman who had given Angelica a firm Catholic background. Deeply distressed, Angelica's father took his daughter to the small village of his birth, in the Bregenz forest, where they sought to recover from their grief by working on the decoration of the church. This so pleased the Cardinal Bishop of Constance that he commissioned work for his house, and sat to Angelica for a portrait.

The Kauffmanns could not forget Italy, however, and when

their spirits were somewhat restored, father and daughter again moved south. They stopped at Montfort, to paint portraits of the Count and his family, and it was here that Angelica's first romance flowered. A young musician in the household wanted to marry her, but it would have meant giving up painting for opera. She seems momentarily to have been tempted by the glamour of a musical career; according to her second husband, Antonio Zucchi, it was this romance which she recalled later in an allegorical painting, *A Female Figure allured by Music and Painting*, which appears to have been done in Florence,[19] and the young musician was no doubt the poet in *Orpheus and Eurydice*, one of her many prints in the British Museum. But, passionate as her first love may have been, it did not finally deter Angelica from painting.

Father and daughter arrived in Florence in June 1762, armed with letters of introduction. While looking for a house to rent, the Kauffmanns are thought to have stayed at the *pensione* run by a Mrs Hadfield, with whom they became friendly and whose daughter Angelica later took under her wing in London. They must also have met the ubiquitous Horace Mann.

In Florence Angelica, then just twenty-one, was determined to work in the galleries, copying the paintings. Permission cannot have been easy to secure, for in those days there was much resentment and suspicion of women artists, but she bombarded the Soperintendente of the Uffizi with her requests, until she was given a room to herself in the gallery, where she could concentrate without the noise of visitors or the inquisitiveness of other students, and where she could even work until late in the evening, by candlelight. She began tirelessly to make copies, both in chalk and in pencil, of the great masters, of which she contrived to sell enough to get a living for herself and her father. At the same time she was ready, for a modest fee, to paint portraits of both the Florentines and their foreign visitors, and she also began doing historical paintings which found a ready sale. The constant copying in the Uffizi seems not to have lessened her gift for painting from life, and later, in Rome, she was able quite remarkably to develop her style in the direction of the neo-classical.

[19] Clara Louise Dentler, *Famous Foreigners in Florence* (1964).

Angelica had obviously not wasted her time in Florence, since she was already well known in Rome when she arrived there a year later. Moreover, she had developed into charming and graceful womanhood. In Florence she had met both Benjamin West and the German artist, J. F. Reiffenstein, and they gave her introductions to people in Rome. In 1763 the art gossip and English antiquarian, D. Crispin, wrote from Rome to his friend James Grant, who had recently made the Grand Tour:

> We have a little German Paintress lately come here from Florence, where she had acquired great Fame, and whose Pencil, they say, would merit no less Patronage than her Person, her Voice, her Manner, and her Sense, are sure to please. She is but nineteen [*sic*], has made some Copies at Florence deemed excellent, has brought one with her of a Rembrandt, of great Merit, has done some portraits very well. . . . She sings and understands musick well. . . .[20]

In Rome Angelica again met Benjamin West, for in the National Portrait Gallery in London there is a portrait drawing signed 'Mr West—Drawn by Angelica Kauffmann, 1763', and there is an unfinished sketch for this in the Vallardi album.[21] The international artists in Rome then included Batoni, Hamilton, Dance, Maron, Blanchet and Morrison, and no doubt she met them all, for Roman artists at this time kept open house in their studios, welcoming prospective buyers and fellow artists.

An important figure in the Roman world was J. J. Winckelmann, of whom Angelica painted one of her best portraits. Winckelmann, a poor German schoolmaster, self-taught in Greek and Latin, had become the supreme arbiter of artistic taste in Italy, and the prime mover in the neo-classical revolution. In Rome he had found a patron in the scholarly collector, Cardinal Albani, who took him into his household, and gave him the opportunity to write *The History of Ancient Art,* published in

---

[20] Unpublished letter in the Scottish Record Office, Edinburgh. Ref. GD 248/49/2.

[21] This sketchbook of her early neo-classical drawings, done between 1762, and 1766, is now in the Victoria and Albert Museum, London. The drawings were given or sold to Giuseppe Vallardi, a dealer in Milan deeply interested in the neo-classical movement, in 1800, when Angelica was living in Rome. He arranged them in a bound volume for sale, and they passed through the hands of three buyers, before, in 1927, they were bought by the V. & A.

1764, which made his name. On 18 August in that year he wrote that his portrait had been painted

> by an unusual person, a German paintress, for a friend. She is extremely good at oil portrait, and one of me cost 30 Zecchini: it is a half-length seated figure. . . . The young woman of whom I speak . . . was at an early age brought to Italy by her father, who is also an artist; she thus speaks German ever so well, like one who was born in Saxony. She also speaks fluent French and English, so she paints all of the English who visit here. She can be thought beautiful, and sings as well as our best virtuosi. Her name is Angelica Kauffmann.[22]

Angelica was undoubtedly influenced by this lover of all things Greek. Winckelmann believed that in painting, though colour might be necessary to heighten form, beauty and purity of line lay in the form itself. He attached particular importance to the nude in sculpture. But in painting the nude figure, Angelica was at a distinct disadvantage, for it was unheard-of for a woman to attend a life class to study a live male model. She could only observe the Greek masterpieces in museums and palaces.

Winckelmann's doctrine of neo-classicism was later spread in England by Angelica and by Benjamin West. The historian himself came to a dreadful end, murdered in 1768 at an inn between Vienna and the Italian border by a fellow traveller, to whom he had unwisely shown some fine gold Greek coins.

The first drawing in the Vallardi album of Angelica's sketches is of Virgil's tomb, rather picturesque and overgrown, on a hill at Posillipo, near Naples. It must have been done during her first visit to Naples, when she was busy painting portraits of English visitors making the Grand Tour. Her English by now was so fluent that she could converse easily with the young sons of the British upper classes who wished to take home a portrait or possibly a painting, at the comparatively low price the exchange with the English pound afforded. (Dr Johnson thought, however, that portrait painting was an improper employment for women, and staring in the eyes of men indelicate in a female!)

Angelica and her father returned to Rome in April 1764. It

[22] J. J. Winckelmann, *Briefe* (Berlin, 1954).

must have been at this time that she met the painter Nathaniel Dance (knighted later as Sir Nathaniel Dance-Holland), who had come to Italy in 1755. Dance was a well-to-do connoisseur as well as a talented artist, son of a well-known architect, George I. Dance, who designed the Mansion House in London. He observed Angelica's fresh complexion, blue eyes, good features, and good-humoured and vivacious personality, and fell deeply in love with her. No doubt she was fond of him too—as perhaps she was of others; but she did not, as Dance believed, consider herself engaged to him, nor would she agree to marry him later when they were both in England. It would of course have been a suitable match; but Angelica was young, successful and much admired, and must have felt the world was at her feet. She had her father to take care of all her affairs, and may well have felt that she was not ready for marriage to an English gentleman.

In an exhibition of Nathaniel Dance's paintings, held at Kenwood House, Hampstead, in 1977, one saw the influence on him of the years spent in Florence and Rome. He painted Angelica lovingly but not apparently without truth: indeed, he gave her a *retroussé* nose, as other portraits do not. She was not exactly beautiful, he said, but had such an engaging personality that people were greatly attracted to her. They would have made a handsome pair, for in his self-portrait he has a strong face, sensitive and very attractive.

Later, in 1808, George Dance, Nathaniel's brother, summed up some of the gossip in connection with Nathaniel for Joseph Farington, member of the Royal Academy and involved in its management, who recorded in his diary:

At Rome He [Nathaniel Dance] became acquainted with Angelica Kauffmann and became so enamoured of Her, she encouraging His passion, that when he came to England, whither she also came, it was settled between them that they shld marry.—But in England she became acquainted with Sir Joshua Reynolds, who showed Her much attention, & it is supposed that she looked to Him, expecting that He wd. offer Himself to Her. Her reception of Dance having now become more cold, & Her intercourse with Sir Joshua being noticed by Him, He remonstrated with Her in such a manner that she complained of His temper & assigned that as a reason for now refusing to marry him—His passion for Her was extreme & he engaged His Father to write to her, but all wd. not do. Her resolution remaining unaltered.—[George] Dance sd she never was beautiful but there was something amiable & feminine in Her appearance that engaged people to Her.[23]

The depth of Dance's dejection when he was refused by Angelica can be seen in his cruel caricature of Angelica with his supposed rival Sir Joshua Reynolds, Reynolds holding up his hand as an ear trumpet to a deaf ear. Dance later married and acquired great wealth, becoming a baronet in 1800, and was for many years Member of Parliament for East Grinstead. One of his best works was an excellent portrait of Captain Cook at Greenwich Hospital; it seems a pity that he gave up painting.

In July 1765, Angelica and her father had journeyed from Rome to Bologna, and in October they arrived in Venice, where Angelica must have spent some time with the Veroneses, the Titians and the Tintorettos. She was befriended by the wife of the English Resident there, Lady Wentworth, who then took her to London as her protégée. Poor Joseph Johann, who spoke no English, was left behind for the first time, though Angelica wrote to him regularly until he joined her a year later. In July 1766 she wrote that, contrary to her expectations, she had found the English very kind and forthcoming, and particularly the gentlemen!

The first picture by Angelica Kauffmann to be shown in London was *Portrait of a Gentleman*, in the Exhibition of Free Artists, in 1765. This was of the famous actor, David Garrick, who had been in Rome and Naples with his wife in 1763 and early in 1764; Angelica's portrait of him could have been painted in either place. The artist Henry Fuseli, one of Angelica's admirers, wrote in 1764 to his father in Zurich: 'I do not remember ever having seen a more beautiful portrait than that of the actor David Garrick (who is now in Naples) from the hand of

[23] Entry for 6 January 1808, *The Diary of Joseph Farington*, ed. James Greig, vol. IV (1924).

Angelica.'[24] Garrick himself was not unaware of her charms. He wrote the following verses whilst sitting for his portrait:

> While thus you paint with ease and grace,
> And spirit all your own,
> Take if you please my mind and face
> BUT LET MY HEART ALONE.[25]

Angelica had been fortunate in the friends she made in Italy. Finding her in London, Lord Exeter, who bought some of her best work, immediately introduced her to Reynolds, whose paintings she greatly admired. As she wrote to her father, 'Mr Reynolds is the finest of them all, a very great master. He has a flying pencil which gives a fine effect of light and shade.'[26] Reynolds in turn appreciated her talent and enjoyed her charming company. He suggested that he should paint her portrait, and she his. The gossips soon got to work on the friendship, but it is doubtful if Reynolds ever had serious intentions of marriage.

Meanwhile the talented, impetuous, slightly unbalanced Fuseli had fallen in love with Angelica and proposed marriage. She refused him, and, as always, continued to give her attention to her work. She was meeting the most interesting people in London, from the playwright Oliver Goldsmith to the Princess of Wales, who visited her whilst she was working on the portrait of Princess Augusta, elder sister of George III. This gave a lead to members of society wanting their portraits painted. She became a founder member (one of the only two women members) of the Royal Academy, and sent four paintings to the first exhibition in 1769. In 1770 she executed the four oval paintings for the ceiling of the Royal Academy chamber, then in Somerset House; these were moved to Burlington House when the Royal Academy moved there. Two years later she began etching and engraving, and at this time produced many paintings for the interiors of the London houses which Robert Adam was designing. In addition it was in England that she began in earnest her series of historical paintings. Although the figures depicted in these may seem to be sentimental and to lack individuality, she

[24] Dorothy Moulton Mayer, *Angelica Kauffmann R.A.* (1972).
[25] Percy Fitzgerald, *The Life of David Garrick* (1899).
[26] Mayer, op. cit.

was the product of her time in interpreting classical scenes in this way, and there is a grace and charm about her work which is recognizably individual. Her panels for house decoration are highly successful, more especially when she had developed her own style fully.

Success came to her in these years in England in spite of a serious blunder she made. In 1767, having refused Fuseli's proposal, she fell in love with a Swedish Count de Horn, who lived at Claridge's, was elegant, rich and intelligent, and was welcomed in society. Angelica met him at the house of Dr Burney, Johnson's friend, and readily took at face value a tale he told, that only an immediate marriage could save him from political allegations in his own country. She married him secretly, as he asked, but when the news came to the ears of the Queen, Angelica was asked to present her husband at Court. He made excuses; about this time the real Count de Horn arrived in London, and the game was up. Angelica's husband was not only an imposter but a bigamist; yet she was forced to pay the sum of money he demanded as his price for agreeing to a legal separation. The royal family showed their sympathy, the King requesting her to paint his portrait, and this brought many more commissions. But it was thirteen years before the false husband died, abroad, in 1780, and Angelica, a sincere Catholic, was free.

In 1781, she married the Venetian painter Antonio Zucchi, who had become an R.A. the year after the Academy was founded. Zucchi had met Robert Adam in Italy, and his brother Giuseppe had accompanied Adam in 1757 on his expedition to the palace of the Roman Emperor Diocletian at Split in Dalmatia. Antonio Zucchi had engraved many of the plates used by Adam to illustrate his findings, published as *The Ruins of the Palace of the Emperor Diocletian at Spalato in Dalmatia*. In middle age he had come to England with his brother. Angelica's father must have encouraged her in the marriage, since he was growing old and was increasingly unwell; and Zucchi, who loved her, though older than she, was an admirable man, 'a proud, reserved man, upright and very highly respected'.[27] It was not a romantic marriage but both were successful artists who did not lack

[27] Fitzgerald Molloy, *Sir Joshua and His Circle*, vol. II (1906).

money, and they were deeply involved in their work.

Soon after their marriage they left for Italy with her father, accompanied by their friends the architect Joseph Bonomi and his wife. In Venice her father became very ill, and died in January 1782. Angelica, who had been so close to him all her life, could find relief only in work. Among the many patrons who came to her were the Grand Duke Paul of Russia and his wife. The Grand Duchess was enchanted by Angelica and by the painting she was completing, *Leonardo da Vinci expiring in the arms of Francis I*, which she insisted on buying. The Grand Duke also ordered two more paintings, scenes from English history.

In the same year Angelica and her husband set out for Rome, stopping in Florence on the way. Perhaps it was this visit to which she referred afterwards as 'the golden days'. After taking a house in Rome close to the Spanish Steps, they went on to Naples. There a message from Queen Caroline awaited Angelica, a pressing invitation to take up a position at Court. She refused, but was obliged to start at once on a group painting of the entire royal family, each figure to be life-size. The exceedingly beautiful, classical arrangement which she eventually completed delighted its owners. The Queen showed her appreciation by the gift of a magnificent diamond cross.

Among other commissions was one from Sir William Hamilton, British Ambassador to the Court at Naples. The erudite amateur archaeologist-diplomat on a later visit, in 1791, asked Angelica to paint his second wife, Emma, Lady Hamilton. She portrayed her as *The Muse of Comedy*, a painting which became Emma's favourite portrait of herself and is now in the Victoria and Albert Museum. Angelica gained from her acquaintance with Sir William and was influenced by his *Second Greek Vase Book*, based on his finds near Naples.

A Mr Jenkins, the chief English banker in Rome, was one of Angelica's close friends and later on it was he who arranged the payments (and possibly the commission too) for a full-length, life-size figure of Mrs Harry Benton. This much-praised painting, for which she received a very large sum, may have been the work she exhibited under the title *Portrait of a Lady of Quality* at the Royal Academy in 1797, after leaving England.

Mrs Piozzi, the former Mrs Thrale, long-time friend of Dr

Johnson, was on a honeymoon tour in 1785 with her second husband, Gabriel Piozzi, when she commented:

> I must not quit Rome however without a word of Angelica Kauffmann, who neither English nor Italian has contrived to charm both nations, and shew her superior talents both here and there. Beside her paintings, of which the world has been the judge, her conversation attracts all people of taste to her house, which none can bear to leave without difficulty and regret.[28]

In January 1788 Angelica was very busy with two commissions—one from Prince Poniatowsky, singer and composer, whose portrait she had painted three years earlier, and one from the Grand Duke of Tuscany, for a self-portrait for his collection in Florence. This is now in the Uffizi. She also painted the Grand Duke himself in full regalia.

A friendship with Goethe, whose portrait she painted whilst he was in Italy, brought great joy to Angelica. Every Sunday morning in Rome he would accompany the Zucchis on an excursion, and Angelica lost her heart to the poet. She was dismayed when he left Italy in 1788, and wrote to him:

> Dearest Friend—Parting from you has filled my heart and soul with grief, . . . except for the dear lines you wrote before you started. . . . In Florence you will have seen many beautiful things which you will tell me of. Zucchi thanks you heartily for your kind remembrance of him. . . . When I know that you are well I will try and reconcile myself to my fate.[29]

In January 1795, however, she was to lose someone she valued more: her husband, Zucchi. Understandably, she was shattered by his death, for he had been a close companion as well as a husband, and had attended to all the practical matters of their life. Again she turned to painting for solace.

The peace of Europe was also being shattered—this time by Napoleon. In 1798 the new Republic was proclaimed in the ancient Forum of Rome. The Vatican, the palaces of the nobles,

---

[28] Hester Lynch Piozzi, *Observations and Reflections* (1789, repr. 1967).
[29] Mayer, op. cit.

the museums and churches were all plundered. The populace was aghast, and Angelica must have been frightened and lonely. She had friends, however, particularly Canova and his circle of artists. She fell ill, and when she had recovered set out with her nephew Anton for Florence, Bologna and Como, reliving the past. She had sent her last religious painting to her father's birthplace in Bregenz, for the church at Schwarzenburg, and it was well received. She returned via Venice in order to visit her husband's family, and thence to Rome. There she died peacefully aged sixty-six years, on 5 November 1807.

She was buried in the church of Sant'Andrea delle Fratte where she had worshipped, and had been known and loved. At her funeral Canova and her fellow members of the Accademia di San Luca carried in homage two of her pictures. The procession of mourners was one of the longest seen in Italy for an artist —equalled only by that for Raphael. A bust of her by Canova, executed only a month before, was placed by the altar next to her pictures. Her body was buried in the third chapel on the right of the church, and, according to her wish, Zucchi's body was later moved to rest beside hers.

Angelica destroyed her personal papers and letters, including those of Goethe, a devastating loss, and the only '*cri de cœur*' is contained in the letter to Goethe when he left Rome. She seems to have been exceedingly self-contained, and did not voice her innermost thoughts, her joys and sorrows. In her long career, during which she met and painted many of the most interesting people of her time, she was blessed with the love and admiration of many men; and despite the unhappiness which followed when her heart ruled her head in her first impulsive marriage, her sorrows were more than compensated by the fact that she was cherished all her life, first by adoring parents, after the death of her father by her husband Zucchi, and at the end by her nephew Anton. In order to succeed as a 'career woman' in an age when women were expected to stay at home, she had to prove herself better than many other highly talented artists—and did. Amongst an enormous quantity of paintings, drawings and etchings, there was some exceedingly fine and lasting work.

VII

A Curious Pair:
The Hugford Brothers
of Florence

AMONG the works of art belonging to the grand ducal family of Tuscany, displayed at a recent exhibition in Florence,[1] was a handsome brass clock, dated *c.* 1700, in an ebony frame. On the back, in the centre of a brass frame elegantly inlaid with flowers, is inscribed *Ingn Huggeford nella Galleria del Gran Duca di Toscana.* The clock's maker, Ignatius Hugford, was an Englishman—a Catholic refugee who emigrated to Tuscany towards the end of the seventeenth century. He had been a watchmaker in London, and when he settled in Florence he was appointed Watchmaker to the Grand Duke of Tuscany, Cosimo III, a position in which he remained for the rest of his life. He seems to have been famous all over Italy, for in 1756 the architect Robert Adam sent his watch to him from Rome to be repaired. As Tuscany was an independent republic the ailing watch ended its journey in the customs, where a payment of five guineas was demanded; apparently Adam had recourse to the long-suffering British Envoy, Sir Horace Mann, to whom, as he reported home with youthful arrogance, he wrote 'in so handsome a way as made the Knight Stirr his Stumps to relieve the watch on paying a Zechin or half a Guinea'.[2]

Ignatius Hugford was the father of two sons, Enrico and Ignazio, a curious pair whose fame in the Tuscany of the eighteenth century was to be even greater than his. Both sons were born in Tuscany and lived their entire lives there. One entered

---

[1] *Curiosità di una Reggia*, Pitti Palace, May–September 1979.
[2] Quoted by John Fleming, 'The Hugfords of Florence', *The Connoisseur*, October and November 1958; other quotations in this chapter are from the same two-part article.

the Church and became an Abbot, but made a unique contribution to art; the other was an artist, not a very good one, but as a connoisseur of art he was said to have been unrivalled in Italy.

I

Enrico Hugford, the elder of the brothers, was born on 16 April 1695 in Florence. At the age of fifteen he entered the Benedictine order. After twelve years of solitude and manual work at the monastery at Vallombrosa, he was transferred to the monastery of S. Reparata di Marradi. Here he found the lay brothers had been working in scagliola, made from selenite which they procured from the neighbouring quarries. The Romans had been the first to use plaster made from powdered selenite to produce imitation marble and mosaic; Don Enrico, observing the brothers at Marradi, found a way of making this plaster into a substance so delicate it could be used for pictures. He returned to Vallombrosa as novice master, and in 1743 became Abbot. He was then able to live in the Hermitage at Vallombrosa, known as the Paradisino; there, in a setting rebuilt and decorated to his own taste, he could work undisturbed on his secret methods for the preparation of scagliola.[3]

In 1747 Horace Walpole was writing to ask his friend Horace Mann to commission table-tops for a friend: 'if the original friar can make them I shall be glad,'[4] which suggests that Don Enrico's work had become known abroad. Walpole also ordered several for himself. The scagliola was later to be much in demand in foreign courts, where it commanded large sums; but worldly success did not tempt the Abbot, even when the Grand Duke himself visited him in his cell to offer him a commission. Don Enrico was, however, persuaded to take a pupil, one Lamberto Cristiano Gori, born at Leghorn in 1730, who had previously studied painting under the Abbot's brother, Ignazio Hugford, in

---

[3] There had been earlier attempts to work in scagliola—for example, the table made for Lord Lichfield at Leghorn in 1726, now in the Victoria and Albert Museum—but they were less successful.

[4] *Letters of Horace Walpole*, ed. Paget Toynbee, vol. II (1903).

Florence.[5] And to him and to him only, he imparted the secrets of his art. After the Abbot's death Gori wrote a biography of him—without, however, giving the recipe. He described the process of reducing selenite

> to a friable condition by heat, ground into a very fine powder and then made into a paste which can be rolled out into slabs of various shapes and sizes. When the slab of paste hardens the surface is indented according to the design or pattern to be depicted, and then inlaid with fresh paste mixed with whatever colours are needed for the picture. . . . When completed, the surface of the scagliola picture can be polished and all trace of the inlaying technique is thus concealed. Indeed scagliola pictures have often been mistaken for paintings under glass.[6]

Gori too had many offers of commissions from abroad, including some from England, but he seems to have gone from the monastery to the Grand Duke's Opificio in Florence. It was he who carried the body of Don Enrico back to Vallombrosa in 1771. He himself died in Florence in 1801, and into the grave with him went the Abbot's secret technique.

The monastery at Vallombrosa still has five small scagliola pictures attributed to Don Enrico, a portrait of a monk and four landscape panels; but unfortunately his chief works were lost when the Italian Forestry Commission took over the Paradisino. The elegant columns with Corinthian capitals made by him for the Cappella dei Beati at Vallombrosa remain; apart from these, two small landscape panels now in the Museo dell' Opificio delle Pietre Dure at Florence, bought by the Grand Duke in 1779 from the estate of Ignazio Hugford, are the only certain examples of his work. But the art historian John Fleming thinks there must be other works by him in English country houses, purchased by their owners through Don Enrico's brother in Florence when they were on the Grand Tour. The Abbot's work can easily be recognized, Fleming maintains, from its 'unvarying

---

[5] Gori's portrait drawing of the Abbot, dated 1757, is now the property of the Master and Fellows of St John's College, Oxford.

[6] Relazione dell'Arte di Lavorare in scagliola; e notizie interno. il P.D. Erigo Hugford Monaco Vallombrosa. Lamberto Cristiano Gori (MS degli Uffizi No. 60 vol. 1 ins. 36), quoted by Fleming, op. cit.

colour scheme of salmon-pink, pale blue, light sandy brown and smoky grey, which gives his panels the appearance of *gouache* paintings under thick glass, their surface being exceptionally smooth and translucent', as well as by its technical brilliance.

The Museo dell' Opificio also contains some signed and dated works by Gori, which differ from those of his master but display an even greater technical skill, as shown not only in the subtleties of colour in his flower pieces[7] but in the textured surfaces, often against a jet-black background.

In England the Adam brothers were almost certainly responsible for popularizing scagliola merely as an inexpensive substitute for marble. In 1760, whilst staying with Ignazio Hugford, James Adam wrote in his diary:

> The scagliola is curious, and could be made to answer different purposes; for instance, for columns resembling different marbles, for tables resembling mosaic work, and for most elegant floors, for baths and low apartments, or for linings to any place damp etc.; and likewise for imitating different marbles in cabinet work, and such like things.[8]

Scagliola for practical uses had been imported into England towards the end of the seventeenth and beginning of the eighteenth centuries, but its first recorded manufacture in England was about 1764. The firm of Richter & Bartoli supplied it for the columns and floors used by Robert Adam in some of the great houses he designed.

Unfortunately an Italian named Bossi, who practised in Dublin *c.* 1785–9 as an inlayer of marble and stucco work, has given his name to inlaid scagliola table-tops; whereas Don Enrico Hugford, the initiator of the delicate artistic work, is now scarcely known. The Abbot may come into his own, however, if an interesting attempt to discover the secret of his recipe for scagliola, made in recent years by a Florentine, Bianco Bianchi, should succeed. Having spent years in research, Bianchi's great

---

[7] Two of Gori's flower pictures, elegantly framed, were shown in the 1979 *Curiosità di una Reggia* exhibition in the Pitti Palace.

[8] *The Library of Fine Arts*, vol. II, nos. 9–10, 1831; quoted by James Lees-Milne, *The Age of Adam* (1947), p. 75.

aim is to develop a modern art in original work in scagliola. Meanwhile he devotes himself to restoration, and has become the leading dealer in scagliola table-tops.

2

The brother of Don Enrico, Ignazio Enrico Hugford, was born whilst his parents were in Pisa in 1703, and was baptized in the Baptistery there on 8 April with Cardinal Francesco Maria de' Medici as his godfather.[9] His parents returned to Florence, and at the age of sixteen he began nine years' study under the painter and connoisseur Anton Domenico Gabbiani, whose biography he published in 1762. Through his brother's influence at Vallombrosa, he was commissioned to do much painting there, and his work is chiefly associated with the Florentine and Tuscan churches. By 1737 he had been appointed *professore* at the Accademia del Disegno and was made steward in 1762.

As time went on, however, Ignazio concentrated more and more on his true vocation, that of connoisseur and art historian. We know from the artist Thomas Patch that he was 'well known for judgement and practice in painting as well as for the large Collection of Pictures which he is possessed of'.[10] Since he was also a dealer in paintings, drawings and works of art, not all of his purchases were necessarily to his own taste. Yet in the period from 1730 to 1750 he was buying Italian Primitives—the only collector to do so—and at his death he had in his possession at least two paintings of the *quattrocento* and one of the *trecento*; from which one can deduce that he was indeed a connoisseur. In May 1751, Sir Joshua Reynolds, then in Florence, wrote, 'He has a good collection of drawings, principally of the Florentine masters'[11]—so good that 3,100 items from the collection were bought by the Uffizi from his executor in 1779. Hugford's taste extended also to sculpture, and among his terracottas (whose whereabouts are today untraced) were models by Donatello; he

---

[9] Clara Louise Dentler, *Famous Foreigners in Florence* (1964).
[10] *The Life of the Celebrated Painter Masaccio* (Florence, 1770), Introduction.
[11] *Notes & Observations on Pictures*, ed. William Cotton (1859), quoted by Fleming, op. cit.

also owned wax models of a high quality. He had not only studied and read widely, but was possessed of a superb memory. His best work as an art historian is considered to be his edition, the sixth, of Vasari, published between 1767 and 1772.

What sort of man was he, we wonder? In the charming self-portrait now in the Uffizi, he sits, exquisitely dressed in green satin, stroking his white lap dog—a worldly and amusing person. (He also portrayed himself as a saint, surely with tongue in cheek, in *La Morte di S. Andrea Avellino* in San Gaetano, Florence.) According to his obituary notice in the *Gazzetta Toscana* —he died in August 1778, at the age of seventy-five—he was genial and candid, admired everywhere for his unfailing patience and good humour. Hardly a first-rate painter, even before he became crippled with acute arthritis in the last twenty years of his life, his kindness to his pupils and friends, and the help he gave to unknown painters beginning their careers, made him popular with and respected by other artists.

All the well-known artists staying in, or passing through Florence seem to have known Ignazio, and many of them stayed with him. Sir Joshua Reynolds, Gavin Hamilton, and Joseph Wilton, the sculptor,[12] were among his guests. When Robert Adam came to Florence in 1755, he brought a letter of introduction to Hugford from Gavin Hamilton; and five years later Robert's brother, James, was having his letters directed 'care of Signor Hugford'. Another of Hugford's guests, the artchitect Clérisseau, was to have an important influence on Robert Adam's approach to architecture.[13]

It cannot be denied that Hugford as a dealer occasionally engaged in faking. Writing to Horace Walpole in 1752, Horace Mann remarked: 'Mr Bouverie bought those of Holbein of Hugford, and those of Guerchin of Bondocci, at a very high rate near two years ago. Mr Chute saw them and did not think them all originals, and if they had been not near worth the price he gave.'[14] Sometimes an 'original' might be a copy executed by

---

[12] Wilton spent seven years in Italy, chiefly in Rome and Florence, before returning to England to become, in 1764, Sculptor to King George II, and a founder-member of the Royal Academy (see Chap. V, p. 70).

[13] See chap. VIII.

[14] *Letters of Horace Walpole*, op. cit., vol. II.

one of Hugford's pupils or—as in the amusing story of the Madonna in the Chiesa Collegiata at Impruneta—by Hugford himself.

Apparently the Madonna at Impruneta, one of the most sacred places of pilgrimage in Tuscany, was hidden behind seven veils. The painting had been seen by no one for centuries.[15] Count Richecourt, the governor of Tuscany, wished to see it for himself, after hearing of the miracles performed by the Madonna, and notified Pierano dei Marchesi Giugni of the proposed date of his visit. Pierano determined to examine the painting in advance and in secret it was uncovered. Behind the seven veils was an old wooden board which might once, as it was believed, have been painted. Fearing an exposé by Count Richecourt which would deprive the faithful of their prayers and their belief, Pierano took the board to Hugford. Ignazio painted a *Madonna and Child* in the manner of the early paintings, which remains in Impruneta today as the one believed to have been painted by St Luke!

[15] It stood within the marble tabernacle in The Chapel of The Madonna.

VIII

Robert Adam:
A Scot on the
Grand Tour

TODAY the name of Robert Adam may call to mind only well-proportioned rooms, fine fireplaces in certain old houses, a few gracefully moulded ceilings that have been preserved. In fact, Adam was a man of genius who, after coming under the spell of Italy, worked a transformation in English taste. He introduced a new lightness and elegance into the architecture of the late eighteenth century, and the beautiful houses he designed, with their delicate ceilings and mouldings, their spacious rooms, were to become famous, and to inspire English architects who came after him.

The Adam family, from Kirkcaldy, Fife, was of gentle origin, landed if not titled; it was one of those Scottish families in which the male members, lacking influence in high places, rose to the height of their professions by their own efforts. The strongly puritanical character of their upbringing made such men feel guilty when the pleasures they enjoyed were unearned. Throughout the eighteenth century and even after it, the letters and diaries of successful Scots testify to the necessity they felt of justifying any extravagance or the least trace of dilettantism.[1]

Any Scot who grew up in Edinburgh in the early eighteenth century, as Robert Adam did, received an excellent education based on hard work and with the principle of self-improvement dinned or 'leathered' into him. Robert's family was large, close-

---

[1] Proud as Harold Macmillan was of his Scottish crofter forebears, he once remarked in my hearing that a certain shy but wealthy Scottish politician should enjoy his riches instead of always seeming ashamed of spending money—yet he himself, highly successful politician, publisher, and later historian, could often be seen in the Strand waiting for a bus, even when he was in his seventies.

knit and affectionate, well provided for by his father, William Adam, an architect of no mean ability and a successful business-man at the same time. He named his four sons John, Robert, James and William, and gave his six daughters all equally plain names, in the hope no doubt of saving them from future vanity. But William Adam was highly respected by some of the best brains in the city, which had a flourishing intellectual life, and his puritanism did not keep him from being part of a cultured and interesting circle. A first cousin was William Robertson, the erudite historian and Principal of Edinburgh University, and among the Adams' friends were Sir John Clerk of Penicuik, artist and antiquarian, who made a tour of English country houses with William Adam; John Home, the playwright; Adam Smith, the economist and author of *The Wealth of Nations*; and David Hume, the historian and philosopher.

The decade of the 1730s was William Adam's most productive in terms of architectural works, among them the Royal Infirmary of Edinburgh and Hopetoun House. He had become the leading architect in Scotland. An emphasis on sound construction and an admiration for Vanbrugh were William's chief architectural legacies to his sons, and particularly to Robert, who in other respects diverged so greatly from the architect of Blenheim. When William died in 1748 his eldest son John, who inherited the business and the estate, was twenty-seven; Robert was twenty. Their mother, May Adam, continued to preside over the social life of her 'bairns'; and whenever the sons were away from home they wrote regularly to her. She was a stern Presby-terian for all her affectionate nature, and it was typical of the respect in which he held her that when Robert first brought the atheist philosopher, David Hume, home to supper, he contrived to introduce him simply as 'Davie' without revealing his name. Fortunately by the time she learned who he was Mrs Adam had already found Hume to be 'the most innocent, agreeable, facetious man' she had ever met.

Robert Adam was a popular man all his life, though he was said to be lacking in a sense of humour; he was possessed instead of enormous drive and, later on, of a sense of purpose. His younger brother James, on the other hand, though he set up in business with Robert in London and they remained good friends, was a very different type, a dilettante with a great affectation in dress. Although Robert never married it was not for lack of interest in the opposite sex, as a neighbour of the Adams, Alexander Carlyle, observed years later, recalling that before his departure on the Grand Tour Robert galloped his favourite horse round the green 'like a madman . . . he had been making love to my maid Jenny, who was a handsome lass, and had even gone to the length of offering to carry her to London and pension her there. All his offers were rejected, which put him in a great flurry.'[2]

In 1754 the proposal was made that Robert should accompany Charles Hope, the Earl of Hopetoun's brother, on the Grand Tour. Robert, who wanted to study the monuments of antiquity *in situ* and had been saving and preparing for such a journey for some time, accepted with delight. He could be independent and would insist on paying his full share of expenses—the Adams could well afford it—saving only the cost of a carriage, which Charles Hope intended to buy; but travelling with a member of the aristocracy would be useful as a means of obtaining introductions in Italy. By no means ignorant of the need to create an impression, Robert got the painter, James Norris, to sketch for him a coat-of-arms which, when cut, would be used to seal his letters. He also canvassed letters of introduction from his most influential friends, and took with him a manservant, Donald, to look after him. Whether his father would have approved these preparations is problematical.

Robert's brother James went with him to London at the beginning of October. It was James's first visit to the city and he took the opportunity to purchase some suits of the latest fashion; Robert meanwhile was receiving introductions and advice from the painter, Gavin Hamilton, who had just returned from a lengthy stay in Italy. The brothers crossed to Calais and, as arranged, joined Charles Hope and his coach at Brussels. James left them at Lille to return home, and Robert and Charles Hope proceeded to Paris. There Robert yielded completely to the

---

[2] *Anecdotes and Characters of the Times*, ed. James Kinsley (1973).

necessity of outfitting himself *à la mode*, no doubt pleasurably though he laughed at himself in his letters home.

They then went on quickly south via Lyons and Toulon to Nice, where Robert became much concerned with preparations for the sea passage to Genoa. Having been told that Barbary pirates were an active danger in those waters, he was much relieved to find the province and its galleys under the command of a Scot, General James Paterson, brother of Sir Hugh Paterson of Bannockburn (whose niece, Clementina Walkinshaw, had become the mistress of Bonnie Prince Charlie after the Young Pretender's defeat in the '45 rebellion).[3] Robert had bought a pair of silk sheets in Lyons and he now added a good pair of blankets, which he decided would be needed on board ship, in addition to his topcoat, to keep out 'the cold of the sea air at this season'.

In Genoa, which they reached without incident, Robert made some further additions to his wardrobe. Genoa in those days was noted for its velvet, and to his basic black velvet suits, which could be worn with different coloured waistcoats, he added another, this time of grey. He also sent home to Edinburgh suit-lengths of grey, dark chestnut and light blue velvet for his three brothers, black velvet to make a cloak for his mother, and even 'a vast bonny green uncut velvet' for a suit for his nephew 'Wee Willy'.

By 18 January, after some storms, the sea was sufficiently calm for them to embark for Leghorn. Indeed, it was too calm; there wasn't a puff of wind, and the boat had to be rowed the whole way to Lerici, where Shelley was later to stay. From there they took post-horses and went by road, warmly wrapped up in their chaise, through the Duchy of Massa-Carrara and the small republic of Lucca to Pisa. The winter of 1755 must have been an exceptionally hard one to cause Robert Adam, who had survived winters in Edinburgh with the easterly 'ha'ar' blowing in off the North Sea, to write that in Italy it was 'so bitterly cold that nothing but withered myrtles, frozen oranges and blasted evergreens were visible'. Arrived at Pisa, he persuaded Charles Hope that they should go on at once to Leghorn where he thought it

[3] See chap. IV.

might be warmer and where he hoped to find letters from 'Auld Reekie'.

Leghorn was by no means a smart social centre, but Hope and Adam found the British Consul there—a Scots gentleman named John Dick, who was a friend of James Boswell (with whose help he later claimed a baronetcy)—an agreeable man. The Consul, Robert wrote, was 'esteemed by all for his hospitality, genteel spirits and sweet behaviour . . . with a very agreeable woman for his wife'. Leghorn was so agreeable altogether that they stayed on to enjoy the opera season. After one opera performance Robert wrote to his sister Nelly that he experienced 'a certain feeling and transport I never felt before, though I did not know the words, consequently received no assistance to my feelings from the meaning or passion expressed in them'; he advised her to learn 'Italian airs'.[4] Towards the end of January the two Scots made their way back to Pisa, where Charles Hope took a box at the opera for the season; this they used every evening during their stay, during which the 'enjoyment of unearned pleasure' continued.

In those years Pisa was a winter resort as well as a summer watering place for the Tuscans, and there were gay crowds in the cafés and shops—and at the opera on that first night:

> We soon cast our eyes towards a very pretty girl dressed in masquerade who went through the whole boxes in the house to pay her respects to the other company, a privilege all Masks have. She sometimes pulled off the mask from her face and showed it, superior in expression, pleasing smiles and agreeable features to any I have seen whilst its prodigious delicate shape and thorough-bred manner made us cock our ears and make enquiries about her. We soon found her to be of no small rank, being the nearest surviving relation of the Medici family. Her own name, Mary of Medici, but being married to a gentleman of the Customs of Pisa she is now called Signora Gianni.

Next day they were taken to the so-called Casino, which was a public coffee-house 'for the best ranks of people and quality

---

[4] John Fleming, *Robert Adam and His Circle* (1962); quotations in this chapter, where not otherwise acknowledged, are from this source.

Enrico Hugford portrayed by his pupil Lamberto Gori.

A landscape in scagliola by Enrico Hugford, bought in 1779 by Grand Duke
Ferdinand III, and now in the Museo dell' Opificio delle Pietre Dure in Florence.

Robert Adam, by an unidentified painter.

John Ruskin as he looked
on his first visit to
Florence in 1840, drawn
by S. Richmond.

Drawing made by Ruskin
in 1874 of a corner of
San Martino, the
cathedral of Lucca.

who game, dance or walk about and see others so do'. Here they met the beautiful Signora Gianni, and were not deterred by the knowledge that she was a married woman. Robert complains in writing home that Charles Hope had the advantage, for 'he gibbers in Italian and was soon in close conversation whilst I stared but could say nothing. Think how I cursed Italian and all foreign languages!' Hope asked the lady if they might call upon her in her box at the opera, and Robert wrote later: 'At the Ball the night after, I had the honour and happiness to dance many minuets with her, as indeed I did with all the Quality of Pisa— some dozen at least.'

Having the entrée now to the local nobility, the serious Robert was thankful that he had ordered all those suits in Paris and Genoa. He was enjoying the social whirl in a way and to an extent that he had never done at home. Life was opening up wonderfully and there would be plenty of time later to give his mind to the study of Italian architecture. Indeed, in his first year abroad it was instinct rather than intellectual interests that governed Robert Adam's activities. He had, however, promised to send his friend John MacGowan a description of the Leaning Tower, which (writing to his mother and sisters) he found 'a horrible but astonishing object. It leans over so much that you can't help thinking it is to tumble down every moment and gives you a sensation not at all pleasing.' But even after frequent visits to the Duomo and the Baptistery, superb white marble buildings standing in their greensward, Robert Adam had not a word to say about their beauty.

On 30 January Robert Adam and Charles Hope arrived in Florence. The city was gay with Carnival, and they needed no prompting to buy masks and 'other appurtenances' and join in. A Scot, Colonel Milne, who owned mercury and vermilion mines near Lucca, gave a ball at which Robert danced with all the ladies he wished to, though he thought the country dances 'shockingly bad'. He later wrote to his mother and sisters in grey wintry Edinburgh what purported to be a complete account of the festive weeks that followed.

As Horace Walpole had found to his astonishment some years previously, two weeks were given up entirely to the Carnival festivities. At first the proceedings were sedate enough: one night a play, the next an opera and then a ball. But later the excitement mounted and propriety became a little shaky. Every single person, high or low, was masked, and coaches paraded through the streets from three in the afternoon 'until six o'clock struck from the campanile of the Palazzo Vecchio'. Off went the revellers then to another masked ball, watched no doubt by great crowds of their less fortunate or less indulgent fellows. The nightly balls ended normally at midnight but towards the end of Carnival they continued into the early hours, and at the concluding ball dancing went on until dawn. Robert was proud to have danced with the best-looking of the nobility and with 'the greatest Whores'. The Countess Salins, whom he had previously described as 'the fat daft wife' of the Army commander-in-chief, he now found worthy of care, as she provided an excellent supper every night of the dancing in Horace Mann's box at the theatre. Robert ate well of this repast, though he referred in some derision to his hostess as 'an old daft frolicsome jade, dressed out with wings and veils and short aprons and the Lord knows what all'.

Mann, as His Majesty's Envoy to the Grand Duke of Tuscany, played generous host in his box at the theatre and at his house, Casa Manetti; he also took Robert and Charles Hope to meet the Governor, Count Richecourt, and various titled Englishmen staying in Florence at the time. Curiously, however, he mentioned neither Robert nor Charles in his almost daily correspondence with Horace Walpole—perhaps, it has been suggested,[5] out of snobbery, since Robert had come with a letter of introduction to the sculptor Joseph Wilton, then living in Mann's guest house, and sculptors at that time were considered not quite the social equals of diplomats.

Robert had also brought a letter of introduction from the painter, Gavin Hamilton, to Ignazio Hugford, painter, connoisseur and dealer, who guided him in the purchase of some drawings (the prices of paintings were too high for him); he was lucky enough to acquire sketches by Michelangelo, Guido,

[5] By John Fleming in his biography of Adam, cited above.

Raphael, Correggio and Giordano. It was through Hugford that he came to the turning point in his tour, and also indeed of his career: his meeting with the French architect Charles-Louis Clérisseau (1721–1820). This man had, as Robert wrote to his family, 'the utmost knowledge of architecture, of perspective, and of designing and colouring I ever saw or had any conception of.' Clérisseau, he said, 'raised my ideas. He created emulation and fire in my breast.' Through the Frenchman he could 'already feel a passion for sculpture and painting which before I was ignorant of, and I am convinced that my whole conception of architecture will become much more noble than I could ever have attained by staying in Britain.'[6] Clérisseau in fact brought Robert Adam to the most advanced thinking in architecture, the most modern appreciation of style—though it was a style based on the classical.

Robert had now to choose between social life and a period of study and work with the Frenchman. He did not hesitate. He knew he must visit the antique ruins and sketch every detail; to do this he had to go to Rome. Clérisseau, to his delight, agreed to go with him. Robert would pay him a salary, and provide him with accommodation; the Frenchman would act as master of perspective and drawing, instruct Robert in these arts and also give him copies of all the drawings he himself had made from the antique. As they made their preparations to leave Florence, Robert continued, with Clérisseau and Joseph Wilton, to study the Tuscan architecture. This too he viewed with new acuteness, writing to his brother James that it was, 'though a little heavy . . . composed of parts far from disagreeable, with doors and windows no less ingenious than agreeable.'

In Rome it became obvious that he must come to a parting with Charles Hope, as it were breaking his contract. In any event Charles no longer wished to act as Robert's sponsor in society, so they went their separate ways without rancour. Robert found very suitable lodgings in the Casa Guarnieri, which had long been patronized by the British nobility. He had an apartment with a bedroom of some size for himself, a smaller one for Clérisseau, a hall where he could set up tables for draughtsmen,

---

[6] Letter to James Adam, 19 February 1755, quoted in Fleming, op. cit.

a dining room and a room for his servant Donald.

From the very start, Robert had a remarkably well-balanced approach to his career. While studying intensively with Clérisseau the art of designing beautiful buildings, he at the same time made provision for having all the detail of the classical structures in Rome (as of the medieval in Florence) at hand to refer to, employing draughtsmen to make the hundreds of copies he would take back to Britain with him—immense folios which were to become the basis for all the work he did in future. Yet he continued to assume with other artists the air of a dilettante patron of the arts, and to spend enough time in the *beau monde* to make the social connections that would help in securing commissions later, when he set up in business as an architect.

Meanwhile he submitted humbly to Clérisseau's teaching. He was now twenty-eight, and in a hurry to get on, but it was only after a thorough grounding in draughtsmanship that he was allowed by his teacher to move on to a deep study of architecture, and to begin to submit his love of the picturesque to the severe discipline of the classical. It was at this time that Robert met and made a friend of the great Venetian architect, Giovanni Battista Piranesi—'the most extraordinary fellow I ever saw,' Robert wrote. Both men were at a formative stage in their careers, and they went out sketching together.[7]

Although he was in these ways completely absorbed in the buildings of ancient Rome (when he began to study the Pantheon, for instance, he could think of nothing else for days), Robert continued to write regular gossipy letters home, telling his mother how he had glimpsed the Cardinal Duke of York (Bonnie Prince Charlie's brother) driving in his coach from St Peter's, where, in a small chapel, he said Mass every day for anyone who cared to attend. Robert had not seen the Pope, Benedict XIV, who was ill, nor 'James how's he cau'd—the Old Pretender', but he was expecting to dine soon with the Stuarts' physician and hoped to hear there some gossip of the Palazzo

---

[7] A bicentenary exhibition of Piranesi's etchings of the Roman ruins and of his other work, held at the Hayward Gallery in London in 1979, included several of Robert Adam's drawings, because of the influence the Venetian master had had on him.

Muti. His description of this Dr Irvine must have made his Presbyterian mother's hair stand on end:

> a very sensible, clever old man of nearly eighty years who every day drinks his four to five bottles of wine, has a flow of spirits meet for forty years and does not look sixty. The best Whigs go to see him so that it is no stain [to serve the Stuarts] and he is so sensible as not to say or do anything to offend them.

Apparently Robert suffered from migraine, and when the strain of all he was attempting to do and learn overcame him he would be assailed by fierce headaches. When the migraine occurred, he wrote, the Abbé Grant would sit with him and 'chatter till ten o'clock at night', and as soon as Robert felt better they would go out on a round of the 'English houses'.

Robert made several expeditions with Clérisseau to Naples. For his intended visit to Venice and the Adriatic, being in default of transport now that Charles Hope and his coach had gone their own ways, he bought himself a smart new carriage, 'one of the handsomest little chariots I ever saw; painted green and gold, well lined and as good as new. . . . I paid £34 sterling. . . .' He knew the effect he would create when he returned thus caparisoned to Florence, with Clérisseau, two young draughtsmen and the faithful Donald. Sir Horace Mann received him warmly: this was no longer the humble Scots companion of the Lord Hopetoun's brother, starting out on the Grand Tour.

Horace Mann had a nose for class and distinction. Besides, several highly-regarded artists and connoisseurs, as well as Piranesi and Ignazio Hugford, had reported on the remarkably talented work, the original plans and ideas the young Scots architect was producing in Rome, and the aristocratic connections he had acquired. Mann himself spent four hours at his lodgings going over Robert's drawings, and Mann, of course, was the best PRO Robert could have had. Soon all the *cognoscenti* of sophisticated Florence were coming to see him. Robert enjoyed this hugely, and went, on a pressing invitation, to Horace Mann's box at the theatre every night. However, he assured his family that success, which he suspected could be ephemeral, was not going to his well-balanced Edinburgh head.

From Florence he travelled via Bologna to Venice, where in 1757 he made an expedition to Dalmatia. There he and Clérisseau sketched the remains of the Emperor Diocletian's Palace at Spalato (Split—or Spalatro, as Robert continued to call it), which was to have a significant influence on his later work. Nine years later he published in England a folio volume of engravings, by Bartolozzi and others, of his drawings of the palace, which gave a powerful fillip to his reputation.

After three years in Italy, having taken the full measure of his inspiration from Florence and Rome, Robert Adam was ready to begin his professional work. In 1758, he opened an office in London. Slowly he gained confidence in executing the commissions that came to him, and by 1761 his reputation was such that he was made Architect of the King's Works. He withdrew from this post in 1769, when he was offered the seat for Kinross in the House of Commons. But he soon realised he had no future as an MP, or none that would be allowed to distract him from his 'noble architecture'.

Meanwhile his brother James had joined him in the business. James too had made the Grand Tour. Robert had arranged for him to have the benefit of Clérisseau's tuition and guidance when he arrived in Florence, but James was more of a dilettante, and although he stayed in Italy for three years, he spent most of the time enjoying the social life of Rome. What he did learn, however, with Ignazio Hugford's guidance, was how to judge painting, and his collection of works of art would certainly, if sold, have paid for the whole of his tour. At Robert's instigation, James was the means of acquiring the drawings of the great connoisseur, Cardinal Albani, nephew of Pope Clement XI, on behalf of King George III. But although he and Robert were partners in the business and were always referred to as the Adam brothers, most of the architectural talent and flair, as well as the drive, came from Robert.

In his best work Robert Adam was moving away from the grandeur and the rather heavy splendours of the Queen Anne and earlier periods, away from Palladian towards a neo-classical line which was light and airy and simple, with beautiful adornments and motifs, whilst yet retaining, especially in his interiors, a fine sense of proportion. He and James also designed elegant furniture, ceilings and fireplaces to grace the noble apartments, and included exquisite wrought-iron work.[8] Robert's genius found free expression in Syon, Osterly, Harewood, Kenwood, Kedleston and other great houses. The octagonal Shakespeare Temple which he designed for David Garrick (as well as adding a new front to his house at Hampton) Zoffany has immortalized in one of the most superb of his conversation pieces. For these and other architectural wonders one is eternally grateful to the influence of Italy, which added new dimensions to Robert Adam's artistic understanding and produced buildings which today are part of our most precious cultural heritage.

---

[8] Only Robert Adam's occasional use of scagliola (see chap. VII) for pillars—a mock marble instead of the real thing, as at Kenwood, for instance—seems, to this inexpert observer, out of the true classical tradition. For the floor of the anteroom at Syon, without the heavy veining and polished like marble, the scagliola is exciting, and for inlaid table-tops of fine workmanship it is admirable; but the Kenwood pillars have none of those 'vague and veined labyrinths, which Ruskin described as 'notably attractive to the human mind'.

IX

Ruskin in Tuscany: 'A Seeing and Feeling Creature'

'I had . . . vialsful, as it were of Wordsworth's reverence, Shelley's sensitiveness, Turner's accuracy, all in one.'[1] What sort of man could boast of such versatility? John Ruskin, critic, artist and art historian, architectural draughtsman, poet, social reformer, amateur geologist, and much, much more, was a romantic with a precise scientific strain. He could turn accepted ideas of art on their heads, could contradict himself and still be interesting. And although his own works are no longer much read, the many recent books about him have led to a reassessment and a revived interest in him both in England and America.

An isolated, precocious child, Ruskin grew up under the unnaturally strict surveillance of a stern Scottish mother, who gave him his early education and read the Bible with him every day until he went to Oxford. John James Ruskin, his father, partner in a firm of wine merchants, was the less dominating of the parents, but his love of literature and shrewd appreciation of art did initiate his son into the world of culture. On his thirteenth birthday Ruskin received a copy of Roger's *Italy*, illustrated by Turner. Thus began both his lifelong appreciation and collection of Turner's works, and his love of Italy, and particularly of Tuscany. He was later to be critical of the Tuscans for their neglect of their art and their ancient buildings, but his obvious joy in both, and in their landscape, shines through his writings and was to lead to a new appreciation of Tuscany and its artistic heritage.

[1] Ruskin, *Praeterita*, vol. xxxv in *The Works of John Ruskin*, ed. E. T. Cook and A. Wedderburn, 39 vols. (1903–12). Ruskin quotations in this chapter are from this edition unless otherwise indicated.

Apart from the years of his marriage, Ruskin lived at home with his parents throughout their lives. Whilst he was up at Christ Church his mother stayed in rooms near by, and was joined by his father at weekends. But in old age Ruskin recalled that although he had tea with his mother daily at this time, and went to church with his parents on Sunday mornings, 'otherwise they never appeared with me in public lest my companions should laugh at me'. His mother, he said, came to Oxford solely 'that she might be at hand in case of accident or sudden illness. She had always been my physician as well as my nurse'[2]—a circumstance which may have contributed not only to his hypochondria but to the manic-depressive psychosis which gripped him in later life.[3]

Oxford opened up a new world of friendship, and of contact with other minds, after his claustrophobic upbringing. At the breakfast table of Dr Buckland, a Canon of the Cathedral, he met the leading scientific men of the day; Henry Acland, who as an undergraduate then, and later as Professor, introduced the study of physiology to the University, was to remain a lifelong friend. Rather touchingly Ruskin says, 'muff or milksop I might be', but he could hold his own, was able to move among his peers and even to entertain, aided by the excellent wine his father provided.

Ruskin was twenty-one when in 1840 he came to Italy, with his parents, for the first time. His account in *Praeterita* of entering Tuscany over the river Magra, in flood, is vivid:

> . . . the rain with wild sirocco came on; and there was a pause at the brink of one of the streams in rather angry flood, and some question if the carriage could get through. Loaded it could not, and everybody obeyed these orders and submitted to the national customs with great hilarity, except my mother, who absolutely refused to be carried in the arms of an Italian ragged opera hero. . . . Out of the carriage she would not move, on any solicitation;— if they could pull the carriage through they could pull her too, she said; my father was alike alarmed and angry, but as the surrounding opera corps de ballet seemed to look on the whole thing rather

---

[2] *Praeterita*, op. cit.
[3] See R. H. Wilenski, *John Ruskin* (1933).

as a jest . . . than any crisis of fate, my mother had her way; a good
team of bare-legged youngsters was put to, and she and the
carriage entered the stream with shouting. Two-thirds through,
the sand was soft, and horses and boys stopped to breathe. There
was another and really now serious remonstrance with my mother,
we being all nervous about quicksands. . . . But stir she would not;
the horses got their wind again, and the boys their way, and with
much whip-cracking and splashing, carriage and dama Inglese
were victoriously dragged to dry land.

He has brought the whole scene, and his parents, alive for us.
We feel as though we already know the dominating Scots-
woman and the anxious husband, whilst the son enjoys it all and
in remembering it shows an innate sense of humour, with kindly
laughter at his own family and the British attitude to the Italian
peasants.

Continuing, they took time before entering Massa to 'walk
up the dazzling white road to the lower quarry'; then they were
on the road to Lucca. Ruskin's initial impressions of Lucca, set
down in old age, were confused with those of his next visit,
without his parents, in 1845; but he never forgot '. . . the first
sight of Pisa, where the solemnity and purity of its architecture
impressed me deeply; yet chiefly in connection with Byron and
Shelley.'

Looking back, he says he feels ashamed of the impressions of
his first visit to Florence as recorded in his diary. He was much
struck by Piazza della Signoria (then his mind wanders to Piazza
del Duomo):

> the square of the statues . . . as it opened from the river with the
> enormous mass of tower above . . . and luckily, coming on it at
> the south-east angle, where the gallery round the dome is com-
> plete, got nearly run over before I recovered from the stun of the
> effect. Not that it is good as architecture even in its own barbarous
> style.

He was disappointed in the great galleries of the Uffizi and Pitti
Palace, perhaps not having been prepared for the quantities of
religious art. One master—'M. Angelo'—was different: 'I saw
at once in him that there was emotion and human life, more than

in the Greeks; and a severity and meaning which were not in Rubens.' And even on this first visit, as often thereafter, he made drawings, for example of the Ponte Vecchio, with its shops and the buildings beyond, that render accurately the 'vague floating quality of the chief masses'.[4]

When they moved on towards Rome, they stopped in Siena, where (as he remembers in *Praeterita*) he 'had a bad weary headache . . . and the cathedral seemed to me every way absurd—over-cut, over-striped, over-crocketed, over-gabled, a piece of costly confectionery, and faithless vanity'. This was surely a case of artistic indigestion, from a surfeit of works of art and of sightseeing. It is true that the external horizontal lines of green marble interspersed with white, as in the Cathedral at Siena—or, as in Giotto's campanile in Florence, with pink—are a complete change from the more sober façades of Northern Europe. But when the eye has become adjusted to their patterns, and in the stronger light of Italy, they open new dimensions of loveliness in colour and texture. Of course Ruskin did not work from photographs, as art historians now do, but kept going back to the buildings which interested him, each time writing down his impressions as their aspects changed according to the light and the point of view. Later, as his knowledge of the material developed, he was to look at marbles (in *The Stones of Venice*) with a more analytical eye:

> The colour of the white varieties is of exquisite delicacy, owing to the partial translucency of the pure rock; and it has always appeared to me a most wonderful ordinance . . . that all the variegated kinds should be comparatively opaque, so as to set off the colour on the surface, while the white . . . is rendered just translucent enough to give an impression of extreme purity, but not so translucent as to interfere in the least with the distinctness of any forms into which it is wrought. The colours of variegated marbles are also for the most part very beautiful. . . .

The first volume of *Modern Painters*, which had originated in a defence of Turner's later work and developed into a treatise on the art of landscape painting, was published when Ruskin was

---

[4] See John Unrau, *Looking at Architecture with Ruskin* (1978).

only twenty-four. Meanwhile he was improving his skill in drawing, and concentrating on the geological and mineralogical studies which were to find such joyous expression in later visits to Lucca and the neighbouring Carrara mountains.

In the spring of 1845 Ruskin made his first journey to Italy on his own, without his parents. Although he was now twenty-six years old, he had already suffered his first breakdown, and his parents were anxious about the trip; as Turner remarked accusingly: 'There'll be such a fidge about you when you are gone.' Like Byron before him, Ruskin travelled in comfort, but with less baggage and minus the menagerie. He hired a carriage requiring only two horses, the top of which folded back in fine weather, and there was a dickey behind for his valet, George. They bowled along, averaging a hundred kilometres in eight hours' travelling a day. At Geneva he picked up Couttet, the guide his parents had used on an Alpine tour, who coped with customs and staging posts.

From Lucca, where he was staying 'in this comfortable house' (almost certainly the present Albergo dell'Universo), he wrote to his father on 3 May: '. . . I pushed on here today, not because I found nothing either at Magra and Carrara, but because I found too much.' He had revelled in the church at Carrara, 'a perfect gem of Italian Gothic, covered with twelfth-century sculpture of the most glorious richness and interest', in the Visconti fortress (now Malaspina) and the many peaks, each crowned by a castle. Indeed he found 'the mountain scenery so exquisite about Carrara that I saw at once if I began stopping at all, I might stop all May.'

Although it was at this point that Ruskin's interest began to shift 'from landscape painting to figurative art',[5] he was never to lose his pleasure in the countryside around Lucca. As he wrote in the same letter to his father,

You cannot conceive what a divine country this is just now; the vines with their young leaves hang as if they were of thin beaten

[5] Kenneth Clark, *Ruskin Today* (1964).

gold—everywhere—the bright green of the young corn sets off the grey purple of the olive hills, and the spring skies have been every one backgrounds of Fra Angelico. Such softness I never saw before.[6]

He found the people of Lucca 'graceful and interesting', and was immensely impressed by the unbroken walk round the ramparts of the city, 'which commands every way the loveliest ranges of the Tuscan Apennines'.

Ruskin then started to examine seriously the architecture and furnishings of the Lucchese churches. In the twelfth-century San Frediano, he found he could draw in the early morning without disturbing the people at Mass, which was not well attended— owing to the gloom, he thought. He mentioned the 'noble' picture by Francia over one of the altars, evidently in the Buonvisi chapel.[7] After midday he moved on to other churches; in San Romano the Dominican monks encouraged him in his study of the two great Fra Bartolomeos (now in the Guinigi Museum). In the afternoon he sat out in the warm air of the Piazza, once the Roman Forum,

drawing the rich ornaments on the façade of St Michele. It is white marble, *inlaid* with figures cut an inch deep in the green porphyry, and framed with carved, rich, hollow marble tracery. I have been up all over it and on the roof to examine it in detail. Such marvellous variety and invention in the ornaments and strange characters. . . . The frost, where the details are fine, has got underneath the inlaid pieces, and has in many places rent them off, tearing the intermediate marble together with them, so as to *uncoat* the building of an inch deep. Fragments of the carved porphyry are lying about everywhere. I have brought away three or four, and restored all I could to their places.[8]

[6] *Letters*, vol. I in *Works*, op. cit.

[7] This painting was removed later in the nineteenth century, and is now in the National Gallery, London; it has been replaced in San Frediano by *S. Anna adora il Bambino* by Stefano Tofanelli.

[8] Letter to his father, 3 May 1845, in *Works*, vol. I. A recent writer, John Unrau, has commented on Ruskin's 'voracious appetite for visual fact which had sent him scrambling up ladders and scaffoldings to examine a host of minor intricacies before he undertook the large scale drawing' (*Looking at Architecture with Ruskin*, op. cit.).

At San Martino, the Cathedral, he fell in love with the gentle and youthful lady, Ilaria del Carretto, whose effigy lies on her sarcophagus, lovingly sculpted in marble of the softest near-pink by Jacopo della Quercia in 1405. There too he was lucky enough to be able to see the beautiful eighth-century wooden crucifix the Volto Santo, in its *tempietto* of marble with sides of wrought iron designed by the fifteenth-century Lucchese sculptor Matteo Civitali; the crucifix was exhibited only on special feast days in the year. But he was scandalized at the Duomo to see that 'the schoolboys rarely pass the porch without throwing a stone or two at it. (The *great* thing is to knock off the nose; but that is not always possible when the sculpture is high up.)'[9]

From Lucca Ruskin proceeded to Pisa, taking rooms for two weeks on the north bank of the Arno. He studied and drew the frescoes in the Campo Santo, and made notes; but he was appalled at the heedless treatment of 'two frescoes of Giotto torn away at one blow to put up a black pyramid'. He collected fallen pieces from the Baptistry, and studied everything, including the Gothic gem by the river, Santa Maria della Spina. Brooding on 'that strange disquietude of the Gothic spirit that is its greatness', he noted sardonically of the church, 'They want to pull it down to widen the quay; but as they say in *King Lear* "That's but a trifle here".'[10] He was not to be reconciled to the Tuscans' lack of care for their ancient heritage.

At the end of May he moved on to Florence, where he stayed at the Hotel dell'Arno and Gran'Britannia. To his friend George Richmond he wrote on 4 June that he had been in the city for a week without yet entering the galleries, but had been to San Marco and Santa Maria Novella, and the Accademia and the church of the Carmine. After seeing the perfectly preserved works of Fra Angelico in the monastery of San Marco, he wrote home that the centre part of one of the frescoes was as near heaven as human hand or mind will ever go.

There were, of course—there always are—some flies in the ointment. On 17 June he wrote to his father lamenting the lack of peace in Florence: 'The square is full of listless, chattering,

---

[9] Letter to Charles Eliot Norton, 18 August 1874, in *Works*, vol. XXXVII.
[10] Letter to his father, 13 May 1845, in *Works*, vol. I.

smoking vagabonds, who are always moving every way at once. . . . They are paving, repairing, gas-lighting, drumming from morning till night, and the noise, dust, tobacco smoke and spitting . . .' At the east doors, the 'Gates of Paradise', of the Baptistry he was appalled when 'Two English ladies came and stopped before them. "Dear me" said one, "how dirty they are!" "O, quite shocking!" said the other and away they went.'[11]

In fact Ruskin was full of complaints, varying with the state of his health and his swings of mood; but these only add to the pleasure of reading his wonderful letters: 'How comes it that Masaccio heads are half Chinese?' he will exclaim; or,

Tell Palmer [Samuel Palmer, the water-colourist and engraver] with my regards that he is wrong about the *quantity* of colour in Giorgione's landscapes. Their white skies and blues—the coldest— are all painted over a rich cinnamon coloured ground, and the tree greens are laid in first with a fiery brown, and then the green put over. . . .[12]

Back in England Ruskin, who after the publication of the first volume of *Modern Painters* was talked of as a genius ('I feel now as if I had been walking blindfold,' said Charlotte Brontë; 'this book seems to give me eyes'), was in demand socially. Here was no wild, elusive poet of unconventional appearance; Ruskin was sartorially elegant, and led an orderly existence. Behind his teasing, half jesting manner lay a particularly generous disposition, and the wealth to satisfy it. And physically he was attractive, about five feet ten inches in height and appearing taller in his youth owing to his slight build, his smile 'always radiant', we are told,[13] below blue eyes whose gaze could be piercing. (He grew side-whiskers later on, and in 1879 a long beard which gave him the appearance of a sage.) In 1847, encouraged by his parents, the twenty-eight-year-old Ruskin proposed marriage to a Scottish girl, a distant relative, Euphemia Gray, whom he had known since he was a child.

---

[11] ibid. It is interesting that the doors were so dirty even then, before the pollution caused by modern modes of transport.
[12] Letter to George Richmond, 28 June 1845, in *Works*, vol. I.
[13] E. T. Cook, *D.N.B.* entry on Ruskin.

The marriage, which lasted six years, was a disaster, and its eventual annulment on grounds of non-consummation, after Effie had left him publicly for the young Pre-Raphaelite painter John Everett Millais, made Ruskin a laughingstock.[14] But by 1855, going abroad again with his parents, Ruskin declared that he was more at peace than for many years. His health had undoubtedly improved, and during the years of marriage he had written *The Seven Lamps of Architecture* and *The Stones of Venice*. He completed the third and fourth volumes of *Modern Painters*, and despite another breakdown, wrote *Elements of Drawing* and took on the immense task of cataloguing the 20,000 watercolours and drawings bequeathed by Turner to the National Gallery on his death in 1851, Ruskin having been appointed an executor of his will.

Until 1858 Ruskin was relatively happy. Then he fell in love with the ten-year-old Rose La Touche, a young Irish girl of delicate mental balance, whom he wished to marry once she was of age; she, on her part, was determined to convert him to her fervent Evangelicalism, when he had successfully outgrown the Scottish Protestantism of his mother. But Rose died in May 1865, a terrible blow to Ruskin, who in his grief identified his lost love with the lady Ilaria del Carretto on her tomb in Lucca, and with Carpaccio's St Ursula.

In the final volume of *Modern Painters*, published in 1860, Ruskin courageously set out his belief that 'Government and co-operation are in all things and eternally the laws of life. Anarchy and competition eternally and in all things the law of death.'[15] With this declaration, posing as it did a threat to the wealth and privilege of his readers who were enjoying the fruits of the Industrial Revolution, the ceiling, metaphorically speaking, fell on Ruskin's head, and he was ostracised by much of society. His father died in 1864, leaving him a great deal of money, much of which he gave away, feeling it to be an embarrassment. The rest he wished to invest in an idealistic and somewhat impractical agrarian scheme to which each member was to

[14] The story of the marriage has been brilliantly told by Mary Lutyens in her two books, *Effie in Venice* (1965) and *Millais and the Ruskins* (1967), as well as elsewhere, and need not be rehearsed again here.
[15] *Unto This Last*, in *Works*, vol. III.

contribute one-tenth of his possessions. He developed his ideals of social reform in a monthly publication, *Fors Clavigera*, and several hundred members were eventually enrolled in the St George's Guild, each receiving five acres of land. But the project did not flourish.

In 1869, after lecturing successfully throughout the country, Ruskin was appointed Slade Professor at Oxford, and as an honorary fellow of Corpus Christi College, had rooms overlooking Christ Church meadow. After his mother's death in 1871 he bought a house, Brantwood, on Coniston Water in the Lake District, but he also kept the old London family house in Herne Hill for the rest of his life.

Ruskin's constant visits to Italy over the intervening twenty-five years had been partly escapes from maternal tyranny, but in the course of them, Tuscany in particular had cast its spell over him. As he was to say (in *Praeterita*) of that first independent visit in 1845: 'and so to my first fixed aim, Lucca, where I settled myself for ten days—as I supposed. It turned out forty years.' Writing on 3 October 1882 to his friend Miss Mary Gladstone, a headmistress, from Lucca, he was still enraptured by the country:

> Such a walk as I had, too, the day before yesterday on the marble hills which look to Pisa and the sea. It is a great grace of the olive, not enough thought on, that it does not hurt the grass underneath; and on the shady grassy banks and terraces beneath the grey and silver of the wild branches, the purple cyclamens are all out, not in showers merely, but *masses*, as thick as violets in spring, vividest pale red-purplelike light of evening.
>
> And it's just chestnut fall time; and where the olive and cyclamens end, the chestnuts begin, ankle-deep in places, like a thick, golden brown moss, which the sunshine rests upon as if it loved it. . . .[16]

There is an enchanted, and enchanting, quality in these descriptive letters.

After his father's death, Ruskin found a substitute in Thomas

---

[16] Ruskin's letter quoted hereinafter all from *Works*, vol. XXXVII.

Carlyle, the 'Dearest Papa' of his later letters.[17] It was to Carlyle
that he wrote, from Lucca on 5 August 1874, of an encounter on
a walk through the maize fields, where he saw

> the peasants at work, of old Etruscan feature, bidding me good
> evening rightly and quietly. At last at the turn of a path, I met a
> pretty dark-eyed boy of eleven or twelve years old. He knelt
> down in front of me quickly, silently, like a dog ordered to do so,
> on both knees, holding out his cap. There was no servility in the
> action, any more than would be in the dog's—great beauty in it,
> and in the entirely quiet face, not beseeching, but submitting its
> cause to you. I never saw such a thing before.

And again to Carlyle from Lucca on 16 August, of trying to
draw Ilaria del Carretto in the Duomo:

> As I was working there last week, two of the Lucca country-
> women came in, and stopped at it suddenly; then knelt down and
> kissed the hem of its robe. 'Yes, she deserves your kiss' I said.
> They opened their great black eyes, half-frightened, like wild
> pretty animals. 'Che santa è?' said the bravest of them at last.

'Which saint is it?' The lady immortalised by Jacopo della
Quercia was the young and beautiful wife of the governor of the
city, who died in childbirth only a year after their marriage. In
Ruskin's time Italy lived still in an age of reverence, and natural
courtesy did not indicate servility.

Ruskin was influential in turning artistic taste towards the
neglected Primitives, the late medieval, early Renaissance artists.
He got on to the trail of the Greek influence (via the Etruscans,
he thought) in Niccolo Pisano's lovely twelfth-century sculptures; as he explained in a letter (18 August 1874) from Lucca to
Professor Charles Eliot Norton of Harvard:

> . . . The Font of Pisa is native Etruscan. So is that of Pistoia. . . .
> The race has held its own to this day; one of them drove me last

---

[17] Mrs Carlyle said that no one managed her husband as well as Ruskin.
'Carlyle would say outrageous things, running counter to all Ruskin cared for.
Ruskin would treat Carlyle like a naughty child, lay his arms around him, and
say, "Now this is too bad!" ' (quoted in Ruskin, *Works*, vol. XXXVII).

night with the same black eyes that are inlaid on the Font of Pisa—the same sharp ridged nose, a breast like Hercules. . . . The infallible mark of the race and style in the sculpture is straight hair carved in ridges like a ploughed field.

Niccolo [Pisano] has the bossy hair of the Greek Jupiter for everybody, and his great points in the Deposition are pulling out the nails with the pincers, and supporting the weight of the body as it falls. . . . Niccolo, with those pincers pulling the nails out, laid hold of the entire scheme of material and naturalistic art, good and bad; and with the arm of Joseph of Arimathea catching the (dead) body of Christ, embraced Michael Angelo and Rubens and all that they are, and mean.

My Etruscan drives me every evening . . . up the hillside, from which on this side of them, I see as I climb, the Carrara mountains in their purple, and Lucca lying like a crown of gold on the Etruscan plain.

That same summer of 1874 he was travelling to and from Florence, writing on 26 August to Professor Norton:

I am more and more crushed every day under the stupendous power of Botticelli. . . . there are no words for his imagination, solemnity of purpose, artistic rapture, in divinely artistic things; mightier in chiaroscuro than Correggio, brighter in jewelry than Angelico: abundant like Tintoret, and intent on completion like Leonardo—I never saw or thought such things possible till I went into the Academy delle Belle Arti this last time.

Five of his many books dealt with Florence and the region he loved: *Ariadne Fiorentina, Val d'Arno, Mornings in Florence, The Laws of Fiesole* and *The Shepherd's Tower*.

Ruskin was still suffering periods of depression, and gradually, as the above quotations suggest, his capacity for rapture became disordered, and he became incapable of concentration. In 1884 he was well enough to visit Florence for the last time. In the four years after 1885, when he had to resign from Oxford because of his confused state of mind, the episodes of madness came at shorter intervals. Yet between these episodes he was completely lucid—as witness the delightful story of his youth, *Praeterita*, begun at the suggestion of his friend, Professor Norton, which he did not live to finish. He died peacefully at Brantwood on 20 January 1900, and was buried at Coniston, a place in Westminster Abbey having been refused. A passage from *The Stones of Venice* might stand as his epitaph:

> The whole function of the artist in the world is to be a seeing and feeling creature; to be an instrument of such tenderness and sensitiveness, that no shadow, no hue, no line, no instantaneous and evanescent expression of the visible things around him, nor any of the emotions which they are capable of conveying to the spirit which has been given him, shall either be left unrecorded, or fade from the book of record.

X

Robert Langton Douglas:
Art Dealer Extraordinary

'THEY were all robbers,' a cultured Florentine friend of mine once remarked, of the art dealers in Italy—and of course, in a sense, they were. Works of art are far better seen in the places for which they were intended, provided the lighting—and the security, in our day—are adequate, than in museums or the houses of private collectors abroad. But Robert Langton Douglas (1864–1951) was not only an art dealer-connoisseur who bought and sold but an historian and later a museum director who found, loved, and in passing on helped to preserve some of the greatest treasures of Italian art. A robber? Perhaps; but also a 'notable and endearing figure . . . in every way a *galantuomo*', as one admirer noted,[1] and 'a full-blooded Renaissance character', to quote another.[2]

As a boy in Sheffield, attending the Collegiate School near Ruskin's St George's Museum, Douglas had what must have been his first sight of a Renaissance work of art: the serene *Madonna and Child* (c 1435) attributed to Verrocchio, which Ruskin had bought through the agency of Charles Fairfax Murray, one of the first Englishmen of that era to be interested in the early Tuscan painters. (The painting eventually went to the National Gallery of Scotland.) At New College, Oxford, where he read history preparatory to entering the Church, to please his father who was vicar of St Stephen's, Sheffield, Douglas became deeply interested in the relationship between art and Christianity. Ruskin's work was of great importance in leading him to a knowledge of the Italian Primitives, which he

---

[1] The critic Denys Sutton, in *Apollo*, July 1979.
[2] Sir Harold Acton, *More Memoirs of an Aesthete* (1974).

was soon to develop further in the setting of Italy itself.

In the 1890s Douglas gained an extensive knowledge and love of Italy whilst serving as a Church of England chaplain in Leghorn (1895–6), Genoa (1896–8), and briefly in Siena (from Easter Day to Trinity Sunday of 1897). In Florence from 1893 to 1896 he gave courses on Dante, Savonarola, Machiavelli, Michelangelo, and the rise of Christian art, but also found time, it is said, to organize the first game of football ever played in Italy, at Genoa.[3] He moved about the country freely, walking and staying in cheap lodgings in order to see a work of art in a remote church or museum. At Siena, which he particularly loved, he became a friend of the important Zondadari-Chigi family, who owned one of the palazzi surrounding the Campo, and built up a large circle of friends and acquaintances, as well as an extensive knowledge of Sienese painting.[4]

At the end of the decade Douglas returned to England regretfully. By now he was deeply immersed in literary and art-historical work, and was fortunately given permission by Archbishop Temple, to whom he wrote in 1900, to leave the Church. For some years he had been contributing reviews to the *Bookman*. He had also been commissioned by the publisher John Murray to prepare (with S. A. Strong) a new, annotated edition of the massively erudite *History of Italian Painting* by J. A. Crowe and G. B. Cavalcaselle, first published in 1864. The re-editing proved a long and difficult task, but as a result of his labours he was recommended for The Chair of Modern History and English Language at the University of Adelaide. He took up the appointment in Australia in 1900, but his domestic life was turbulent and because of this he resigned in 1902.

The break-up of Douglas's first marriage, to the daughter of a London printer, and the subsequent divorce—a rare thing in those days—caused emotional and financial difficulties for his wife and children. His son Sholto thought his parents incompatible and although he did not get on well with his mother he was

---

[3] Horace Mann, however, writes of a game played at Leghorn much earlier, in 1766.
[4] His eldest son, Sholto Douglas—afterwards Marshal of the Royal Air Force Lord Douglas of Kirtleside—remembers these early years in Siena, when he himself was a small boy, in his memoirs *Years of Combat* (1963), a source for some of the biographical material on R. L. Douglas in this chapter.

grateful for her devotion to the family after the divorce. The vivacity and charm of his father, thought Sholto, led others to indulge his sexual weaknesses. Whilst at Genoa in 1896 Douglas had fallen in love with Grace Hutchison, a naval officer's daughter, who bore him three children and to whom he remained attached. On the return journey from Adelaide, however, he became enamoured of another young lady, Gwendolen Henchman, whom he married in October 1902, after his divorce from his first wife. They had a son and two daughters. Douglas was conscious of his obligations to his children—in all there were to be eighteen of them, of whom eight were illegitimate—and the responsibility for three families, in effect, encouraged him to concentrate on literary work.

His first book, on Fra Angelico, had already been published in 1900. A second edition appeared two years later. Douglas's interest had been captured during his earlier visits to Florence by the art of the Domenican friar, and his book uses contemporary sources to place the artist in the historical context of his times. The accepted interpretation of Fra Angelico (that of Vasari) was as a saint preoccupied with religious themes, who was not influenced by antiquity or by nature. Douglas, however, saw the monk as first and foremost an artist, one of the greatest of all time, who happened to be saintly. He needed revaluation because he painted at a vital point in the artistic development of Florence. Brunelleschi's dome had just been consecrated by the Pope, Ghiberti was at work on the second of his great doors for the Baptistry, whilst Luca della Robbia was sculpting his *Cantoria*. When Fra Angelico came to the convent of San Marco in Florence, Michelozzo was rebuilding the convent for Cosimo I. It was a time when architects and sculptors were having a great influence on painting; but it was an influence that passed unnoticed for many years.[5]

Douglas was fortunate in that Alessandro Lisini, one of the most erudite Italian historians of his generation, had become his close friend. In 1889 Lisini became the Director of the State

---

[5] One of Douglas's contributions to the study of Fra Angelico was to point out that he was the first painter to follow the sculptors Jacopo della Quercia and Donatello in depicting the Christ child naked. The sympathetic representation of the young by Italian artists always struck a chord in Douglas.

Archives at Siena, and because he believed passionately in the value of documentary evidence he made the Archives more freely available to scholars than they had formerly been. Douglas went to Siena as often as possible, and prior to his departure for Adelaide in 1900 must already have done considerable research for his second book, the *History of Siena*, published in 1902. As well as reading and working in the Archives he walked far and wide, using his eyes intently all the time. In his Preface to the *History* he set out his aim to write 'a book which would both be useful to the historical student and also not without interest to the general reader'—for 'whilst her neighbour Florence has had many historians, there is no complete history of Siena in any language.'

He embarked with zest on the history, from the Etruscans and then the Romans, through feudal development as a fief of the Emperor, down to the founding of the Commune of Siena in 1186. After that many battles would be fought, and factions within the Commune would still bicker, but Siena was secure enough to develop her trade and banking, which was to lead her to primacy in international banking for three-quarters of the thirteenth century.

Here Douglas pauses to describe the life and customs of the city in the thirteenth century. He is always readable and lively in his approach, whether he is discussing the heating of houses (he regretted that the Sienese no longer indulged in the 'big fires' they had used formerly), sport, domestic architecture or the excessive application of cosmetics by Sienese ladies. Before glass was used in the windows of private houses, they were made of 'panels of sheepskin or linen made semi-transparent with oil'. He describes furniture and sleeping arrangements—the latter resembled those of the English, but people slept without night-shirts, and two or three in a bed. The Sienese were ahead of us in comfort and cleanliness, washing their hands before meals and even—the more affluent of them—following the habit introduced by the Crusaders of bathing daily. Two Italian recipe books of the *quattrocento* reveal that dishes were complex and sophisticated. Vegetables formed the basis of their diet, and the meats most often served were game, pork and lamb, all of them with plenty of spices from the East. Garlic, Douglas tells us, was an exquisite and aristocratic vegetable'.

He continues to follow the history of the Commune through the centuries, including a chapter on Saint Catherine and another on the times of San Bernadino and Aeneas Sylvius Piccolomini, who became Pope Pius II. Finally he takes us through the two-year siege of the city by the Spanish, when the population was reduced from 40,000 to 8,000; and its eventual subjugation by Florence in 1557.

Chapters on architecture and sculpture follow. Whilst doubting the hand of the sculptor Giovanni Pisano in the façade of Siena Cathedral, Douglas does not underestimate the influence on contemporary art of both Pisanos, father and son, and particularly on the sculptors of Siena. He deals with the classical influences evident in the father's (Niccola's) work, and is convinced that Giovanni had effectively made the transition to Gothic sculpture. In the latter's work he discerns deep personal emotion: 'In his hands marble becomes as ductile and pliable as molten glass. . . .'

As for the famous pavement in the Duomo, Douglas calls it 'a splendid failure' and dates the decline in the art of marble inlay from Beccafumi's work. However, he grants that 'the pilgrim of aesthetic delight will not wander over that wilderness of misapplied genius without finding here and there delightful oases'; the 'Death of Absalom' design is the one which pleased him most.

Douglas's training in history helped him to understand the influence of Byzantine civilization on Siena. He felt that after the fall of Constantinople the Greek nobleman Ranieri da Traviale who came to Siena must have brought artists in his suite, and that they must have settled there, producing a neo-Byzantine culture alongside the native Italian style.

It was when he came to the Sienese painters that Douglas laid himself open to the criticism of experts such as Bernard Berenson, the great American connoisseur. Douglas took up the cause of Duccio with enthusiasm and placed him in his historical context, applauding his superb mastery of colour and his 'curious blending of the results of the Byzantine, Roman and Gothic influences'. He considered him not inferior to the Florentine Giotto, attributing the greater attention paid to Giotto, and to all Florentine art, to the influence of the art historian Vasari and to the popularity of Florence as a centre for visitors. Berenson, in *Central Italian Painters of the Rennaissance* (1897), had declared that there was 'some secret that Giotto possessed, and Duccio never learned'. Douglas, however, maintained that although Duccio's fame 'can never rival that of Giotto, for the simple reason that Duccio was not a fresco-painter', his *influence* was as enduring as that of Giotto, and as that of Giovanni Pisano (by whom he was in turn influenced).

The press received Douglas's *History* well, but Berenson and his friends were critical. F. Mason Perkins (C.M.P.), reviewing the book in *The Burlington Magazine* for April 1903, praised the historical chapters but added that by devoting so much space to Sienese majolica Douglas had upset the balance of the book. He also challenged Douglas's attribution of the Rucellai Madonna to Duccio instead of to one of his school.[6] Berenson himself wrote an anonymous review of the *History* in the *Nation* (10 March 1903) in which he remarked with condescension that the author was capable of 'good work in subjects where finesse or taste are not needed.' Letters which passed between Mrs Mary Berenson and Roger Fry, who had already been critical of Douglas's *Fra Angelico*, reveal the acrimony of the Berenson–Douglas quarrel. Fry even referred to Douglas as 'an outrageous bounder'.[7]

Matters were made worse by Douglas's *Burlington Magazine* article on Sassetta (May 1903), entitled 'A Forgotten Painter'. Tactlessly he began by provoking Berenson, remarking that Sassetta was not listed in Berenson's *Central Italian Painters*. He went on to declare that Sassetta's 'historical importance was greater than his artistic importance; for he was one of the fathers of Umbrian painting. . . .' The article was chiefly valuable for asserting that the exquisite painting in the Condé Museum at Chantilly, the *Mystic Marriage of St Francis*, was by Sassetta himself and not by his pupil Sano di Pietro, as had been claimed.

Berenson waited until the September–October and the

---

6 The attribution of the Rucellai Madonna is still not settled.

7 *Letters of Roger Fry*, ed. Denys Sutton, 2 vols (1972); Fry to Mrs Berenson, 23 January 1902, I Tatti Archives.

November 1903 issues of the same magazine to 'put a shot across his bows' in two long articles on 'A Sienese Painter of the Franciscan Legend'. Loftily ignoring Douglas's article, he compared Sassetta's and Giotto's interpretations of the St Francis legend at Assisi to the advantage of Sassetta who, 'more lyrical and rapturous', gave 'a more poetical rendering . . . than any that the great Florentine had left us'. There was subtlety in Berenson's appreciation, and since in 1900 he had bought from an ignorant shopkeeper the lovely *St Francis in Glory* by Sassetta from the back of the altarpiece of S. Francesco at Borgo Sansepolcro, together with two saints from its front,[8] and had lived with it, it is not surprising that he comments: 'The real meaning of the seraphic existence is surely conveyed here more clearly, more persuasively, more penetratingly than by all Giotto's allegorical frescoes. . . .' Berenson did not allude to Douglas's discovery of the Chantilly Sassetta; it was the editor of the magazine who decided, in fairness, to add a footnote: 'In regard to this picture it is only just to mention that the first to publish its attribution to Sassetta was Mr Langton Douglas, and the medium of its publication was this magazine.'

In the December issue Douglas returned energetically to the fray. In 'A Note on the Recent Criticism of the Art of Sassetta' he disagreed with both Berenson and Perkins on several points, and added fuel to the flames by sarcasm:

> We cannot, in this world at least, look forward to any millennium when there be no quarrels among connoisseurs. But it is a genuine pleasure to all save those who prize such knowledge as they possess because of its rarity—and are out of conceit with it when it becomes common property—to see old differences vanishing. . . . We now find Mr Berenson purged of his former heresy, frankly admitting that there have been great schools of painting which have regarded the 'rendering of tactile values' as of secondary importance.

Berenson, not unnaturally, was upset by Douglas's attacks.[9]

[8] Ernest Samuels, *Bernard Berenson: The Making of a Connoisseur* (1979).
[9] 'The "discovery" of Sassetta by a disreputable critic named Langton Douglas was one of the events that gave Mr Berenson most pain in his life'. Sir Kenneth Clark, *Another Part of the Wood* (1974).

*   *   *

The feud which had developed between Douglas and Berenson continued throughout their art-dealing careers. Although there were many parallels in their lives, their personalities were very different. In appearance they were opposites, Douglas being a big, well filled-out man who always reminded Harold Acton of 'a bishop in mufti', whilst Berenson was small, slender and fragile-seeming. They were both, in their different ways, good-looking, and both were attractive to women, but whilst Douglas enjoyed his family and hated the house without a young child in it, Berenson did not want children and even forced his wife Mary to have an abortion when she found herself pregnant.

Berenson was much poorer in his early youth than Douglas ever was, but both received excellent university educations. Was it, perhaps, the twin disadvantages of being poorer than other boys at school, and of being a Jew among Gentiles, which made 'BB' so ultra-sensitive to the criticisms of Douglas? He may have seen the Englishman as having a head start both socially and financially. The difference in their backgrounds did not affect the way in which both men came to depend utterly on money—large sums of money—for their chosen life-styles. Both liked to 'hold court', BB at his home, the famous I Tatti (which he enlarged and made into a museum-*cum*-library, to be handed on as a study-centre to his old university, Harvard, after his death); and Douglas at receptions in London, and in Europe and America, as he moved around in grand style (while at the same time supporting his eighteen children!). But Douglas was far from having the royal airs which John Walker, for instance—an admirer of BB who worked with him for three years and became Curator, then Director, of the National Gallery at Washington—describes at I Tatti luncheon parties:

> We would all stand more or less in a circle sipping vermouth until the arrival of BB who would greet each in turn, in much the same way that royalty customarily receives visitors.[10]

---

[10] *Self-Portrait with Donors* (1969).

Because their ways of life were so expensive, both Douglas and Berenson eventually had recourse to Joseph Duveen, the foremost dealer in the world's greatest masterpieces of art at that time. Each man had a financial arrangement by which he supplied Duveen with expert opinions. But Berenson in particular recoiled from any mention of the money he so badly needed. He never spoke of it. As Alan Moorehead, who lived near I Tatti and visited the Berensons frequently after World War Two, wrote: 'People no doubt will go on talking dubiously about his dealings with Duveen until the cows come home.'[11]

Both Douglas and Berenson were men of intelligence and wide-ranging interests, fascinating conversationalists and good linguists. Berenson was introspective and fastidious, Douglas was an extrovert. Berenson, with an encyclopaedic knowledge of early Italian art, and acute intuitions, appeared to narrow down and polish his expertise, while Douglas spread his interests more widely and was a more fluent writer.

Success seems to have induced in both men a certain arrogance, Douglas's possibly relating to his personality and background, whilst Berenson's was built up through years of applied intelligence and concentration. At the same time BB's sensitivity to criticism and to being disliked, and his jealousy of other experts, led him to outbursts of vituperative temper when he would 'join battle' with anyone. He refers to it himself in his later writings, and so does Kenneth Clark, describing his first period as an assistant to Berenson. As he grew older BB mellowed, and he was nothing if not honest in judging himself in *Sunset and Twilight* (1964), the diaries which he continued to write, with great clarity, into his ninety-third year.

It is obvious that both men were egoists, as such 'larger than life-size' characters frequently are. BB became a legend in his own lifetime—one of the sights of Europe. Both men felt an intense need of conversation, of verbal communication, right to the end of their lives. Berenson admits that he much preferred his own talk to anyone else's; he talked, it seems, far more easily than he wrote. Did he, perhaps, envy Douglas's facility with the pen? Both men lived to a great age and preferred to spend their

[11] *A Late Education* (1970).

last years in Florence; and each was fortunate, indeed blessed, in finding in later life a young woman to love and care for him: Nicky Mariano for BB and Jean Stewart for Douglas.

Sir John Pope-Hennessy was an admirer of Berenson, but that did not prevent him from telling me that Douglas had been charming and helpful to him. Was there any real need for the feud between these two lovers of Italian art? The aged Berenson himself, in *Sunset and Twilight*, concluded that in his 'chosen field of art criticism . . . almost anything one says can as easily be disproved as proved.'

Let us turn back, now, to 1904, when Douglas put on an exhibition of Sienese art at the Burlington Fine Arts Club in London. Among the wonderful paintings were four panels from one of the two predellas of Duccio's *Maestà* in Siena, together with the artist's *Crucifixion* from Lord Crawford's collection. In his arrangement of the catalogue Douglas showed himself a pioneer in art history, choosing a method of presentation close to that used today. In the same year a large Duccio exhibition was organized in Siena in the Palazzo Pubblico by an enthusiastic young art historian, Corrado Ricci, together with Douglas's friend Alessandro Lisini, who was now Mayor of Siena. Douglas was one of the organisers of this exhibition, which aroused great interest and brought many visitors to the city.

Douglas's work on the history of Italian ceramics was an important aspect of his career, and it is regrettable that he was not able to write the history of Sienese majolica which he projected, since he was a pioneer in this subject and little has been published on it.

He felt that Siena had realized herself more fully in sculpture than in painting. Lecturing on Luca della Robbia and his followers (in whose work Ruskin and Pater had first aroused interest) Douglas deplored the fact that such a great artist as Luca had covered his subtle work 'in a creamy glaze'. Certainly Luca's *Visitation* in Pistoia—to me one of the most movingly tender of all Italian sculptures—would have needed less repair work if it had been executed in marble. To Douglas, Luca was more perfect than either Donatello or Ghiberti. He considered the enamelled terracotta *Resurrection* in the Duomo at Florence to be one of the world's noblest works of art.

The eight marble reliefs of Luca della Robbia's *Cantoria* brought forth great praise from Douglas for their 'wonderful power of representing the vitality, sanity, beauty of happy child-hood', and he hated the idea of their being removed from the position for which they were designed to a museum, the Museo dell' Opera del Duomo.

His 1904 London exhibition of Sienese paintings brought Douglas into touch with great collectors and many museums, and since his writings did not bring in enough money for the upkeep of his several families and the education of his sons, in the same year he set up on his own as an art dealer. This meant, of course, widening his field beyond the Italian masters; and by 1904 the interest of British buyers in Italian art had diminished, so that he had to find buyers abroad. It was at this time that the American J. P. Morgan, among the greatest of collectors, came to his aid with financial backing (news of which caused a rise in the prices of Sienese paintings and majolica). During the next decade Douglas bought as well for the Kaiser Friedrich Museum in Berlin and was responsible for some of the most important acquisitions of the Metropolitan Museum in New York. He was always on the move, visiting galleries everywhere, including the Hermitage in Leningrad.

Italian collectors also came to him. One such was Count Carlo Gamba (of the family of Byron's beloved Teresa Gamba), to whom Douglas sold the *Angel of the Annunciation* from S. Maria dei Miracoli for the purpose of reuniting it with the rest of the panel: happily both are now in the Accademia in Venice. The work of persuading owners to sell, and museums or collectors to buy, could never have been easy, although he had the advantage of being welcomed into the great country houses of Britain and Europe, and he generally got on well with museum directors. One difficult owner, for example, was Sir George Sitwell who had settled in the castle of Montegufoni in Tuscany. 'Sir George never knows his own mind . . . and we have had some very subtle opponents working against us.'[12]

---

[12] Letter from Douglas to Bryston Burroughs, Curator of Paintings at the Metropolitan Museum of Art, New York, 16 May 1911.

Sitwell had originally asked £100,000 for a Perugino master-piece, *The Virgin and Child and Two Saints*. He eventually came down to £30,000 and J. P. Morgan secured it for the Pierpont Morgan Library, New York.

There is no doubt that the connoisseur art dealers influenced both taste in art, and its criticism. For instance, when the French edition of Douglas's *History of Siena* was published (in 1914, translated by Georges Feuilloy), he added a fascinating account of the influence of Simone Martini, who had charmed him, and this made such an effect in France that a school of painting was created in the Midi. Douglas was original in his view of the influence of Sienese art on French painting. It was natural, how-ever, that a dealer should influence his clients by his own taste and knowledge. In 1910, for instance, Douglas procured for the Metropolitan Museum, from Mrs Arthur Severn, two superb figures by Giovanni Pisano and his assistants which had been owned by Ruskin. In 1921 he secured a third sculpture by Pisano for the Museum. He was convinced that these were among the finest works of art ever to have been bought by him.

When war came in 1914 Douglas, always adventurous, dyed his hair and gave his age as forty instead of fifty in order to enlist as a private soldier. After five weeks he was given a commission in the Army Service Corps, and he managed to continue some art dealing. He was in charge of a transit camp in France, where he met his son Sholto, then in the Royal Air Force. In 1916 when Sir Hugh Lane, Director of the National Gallery of Ireland, went down in the *Lusitania*, Douglas was appointed Director of the Gallery. He was able to deal both for the Gallery and for other clients, as his predecessor had done. His contract stipulated that he need spend no more than a hundred and twenty days of the year in residence in Ireland; but there were great problems about the disposal of Lane's collection, so the job was by no means a sinecure.

During the seven years of his directorship Douglas sold the Gallery a number of paintings from his own collection—work by Guardi, Beccafumi and Antoniazzo Romano, and paintings later attributed to Biagio di Antonio, Silvestro dei Gherarducci

Robert Langton Douglas in his late fifties. *Below* Luca della Robbia's 'The Visitation', in the church of San Giovanni FuorCivitas, Pistoia: one of Robert Langton Douglas's favourite works of art.

Bernard Berenson at i Tatti.

The Yorkshireman William Walton who dominated Carrara's marble trade in the second half of the 19th century.

One of the roads by which the 'wicked marble' is carried down the mountains of Carrara.

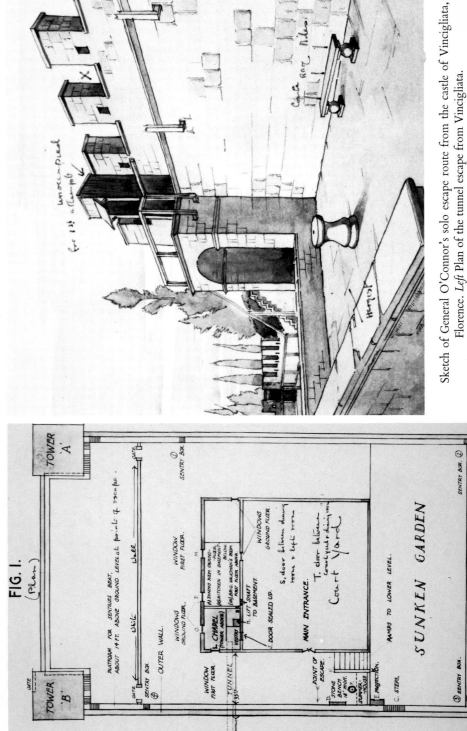

Sketch of General O'Connor's solo escape route from the castle of Vincigliata, Florence. *Left* Plan of the tunnel escape from Vincigliata.

and Girolamo de Benvenuto. Inevitably he was criticized for this, but it appears that he did not overcharge the Gallery. His rather high-handed way of raising money for the Gallery was to ask for contributions from Irishmen in the United States, without first seeking permission from his Board of Directors. He resigned from this post in 1923.

During the 1920s Douglas had several illnesses, but he continued to live handsomely in London and to entertain a great deal. He still had a clientele of wealthy collectors, but complained that it seemed ridiculous that a painting by Duccio fetched only £2,000 or £3,000, whilst 'a flimsy, sugary female portrait by Romney may be sold for ten times that sum'. But if fashionable taste had veered in a direction of which he disapproved, he himself had helped to send it in that direction: he was one of the earliest connoisseurs to be attracted to the eighteenth-century Venetians, and had bought Guardi, Canaletto and Tiepolo. His relations with museum directors remained good, and in 1926 he gave to the Fitzwilliam at Cambridge Guercino's *Betrayal of Christ*; and to the Ashmolean at Oxford Frederick Sandys' *Gentle Spring* in memory of his son Archibald, killed in action in 1916.

In 1928, when he was sixty-four, he had the good fortune to win the hand of Jean Stewart, a young woman in her twenties, whom he married as his third wife. (His second wife, Gwendolen, had 'run off with a Frenchman', his son Sholto observes, thus giving Douglas 'some of his own medicine'.) Then came the Depression, and the rise of the Nazis in Europe, which dealt a serious blow to the art world. Towards the end of the 'twenties and during the early 'thirties one of his chief patrons was his friend Geoffrey Locker-Lampson, son of the poet Frederick Locker. Most of the paintings he bought from Douglas were Italian. But Douglas's financial position became so bad that in 1933 and again in 1937 he had to ask Duveen to advance him money. He continued to travel on the Continent, buying and selling both there and in America. In the 1930s he became a convert to Catholicism, and after the deaths of his first two wives he was able to marry Jean in the Church.

Douglas's most valuable work during these years was the privately printed *Leonardo da Vinci: his San Donato of Arezzo and the Tax Collector* (1944). He had sold this picture to T. T. Ellis in 1933, having been the first to identify the subject. He believed that this small panel belonged to the predella of the *Annunciation* in the Louvre, and that both had formed part of the predella of the altarpiece of the Oratory of the Madonna di Piazza in the cathedral at Pistoia. He maintained that Verrocchio had begun the work in 1475, that his chief assistant, Leonardo, had worked on it until 1478, and that it was completed by Lorenzo di Credi after 1485.

During the 1920s Douglas had built up at considerable expense a fine collection of Sienese majolica, and in the *Burlington Magazine* of 1937 he published reproductions of a few of the antique pieces which he had been responsible for having excavated some years earlier in the garden of the Ospedale della Scala. On one of these was the signature '*ede*', identical with that on the plate in the Victoria and Albert Museum by Maestro Benedetto—who, Douglas proved from documents of 1518 and 1521, was for a long time the official vase-maker of the hospital. He explained that he had copies of detailed accounts for various kinds of glazed earthenware made for the hospital by its own *vasaio* from 1348 to 1596, thus refuting the argument put forward by experts that the Sienese potteries had produced nothing of importance before the eighteenth century.[13]

During the Second World War, having failed to get into the Army to help his country, Douglas settled in the United States, and in the final decade of his life returned to his original career as a writer. In addition to lecturing he produced articles and book reviews, prepared catalogues, and published two books. He reached a convincing conclusion on the way in which political events had changed the art of Siena, showing how in 1430, when Sienese artists were unable to visit Florence because of inter-city war, artistic fashions changed with the 'young bloods of the Sienese studios' becoming nationalistic. This made the

[13] John Pope-Henessy, in *Luca della Robbia* (1980), cites in his bibliography Douglas's 'Cantor Lectures on the Majolica and Glazed Earthenware of Tuscany', 1904.

modern trends then current in Florence unpopular in Siena. Douglas always felt passionately that writers on art should consult historical documents for the background of political and social life. To him medieval and Renaissance Italy were as vivid as his own times.

The firm of Duveen made his life in New York easier by asking him to be a consultant. But as Douglas grew older and his health declined a friend suggested the possibility of his being looked after by the Blue Nuns in their convent at Fiesole, above Florence. In 1951, now eighty-seven years of age, he crossed the Atlantic for the last time.

Thus Douglas spent the evening of his life in his beloved Tuscany, in that beautiful spot with a fabulous view over Florence which so many great artists have depicted. There he finally made up his quarrel with BB, and could indulge his love of pasta and other Italian food, take walks, listen to music—and above all, talk. His brain was still very active and he became garrulous. Once a week Harold Acton's father, Arthur, came over from La Pietra and took him to the cinema, and when John Pope-Hennessy paid him a flying visit, Douglas told him with tears of emotion that Siena had decided to make him an honorary citizen. Pope-Hennessy was horrified at how old he looked; but his mind was still lively and he turned suddenly on his visitor with the comment: 'My, how you've aged!' When Pope-Hennessy told him how useful he had found his fifty-year-old *Fra Angelico*, Douglas bade him use the second edition.

On 14 August 1951, Douglas died at Fiesole; his wife and other members of his family were present, with two Dominican fathers, one on either side of him, as well as some of the nuns. The funeral in Siena was a civic occasion attended by the Mayor, the President of the Intronati, the Director of the State Archives, the Magistrate of the Rural District, and other dignitaries. A medieval procession in vivid Palio costumes, contrasting with the black hoods and gowns of the Misericordia, all carrying flaming torches, accompanied the cortege through the narrow streets between their severe palaces, the populace kneeling revently as it passed.

Douglas's body lies in the peaceful Sienese cemetery of Laterino, just beyond the Porto Romana. The inscription above the city's Porta Camollia might have been written for him: *Cor magis tibi Siena pandit*—Siena opens her heart to you wider than this.

XI

Carrara:
The Wicked Marble

AD ONORANZA DI GUGLIELMO WALTON
CHE A COMUNE VANTAGGIO
AMPLIO IL COMMERCIO CARRARESE
IL MUNICIPIO RICONOSCENTE
POSE IMPERITURO RICORDO
L'ANNO MDCCCLXXIII.[1]

WHY and how did an Englishman come to be honoured here in this ancient town on the fast-flowing Carrione, below the deeply cut mountains of the Apuan Alps rising sheer from the narrow plain bordering the sea? Why this memorial tablet—a tribute unique in this part of Italy—here, on a wall within sound of a water-driven marble-cutting sawmill? But it should not be surprising that the story of Carrara marble leads on from Julius Caesar who opened the quarries to Englishmen such as William Walton who operated them.

The Romans exported the beautiful *marmo lunensis* from the ancient port of Luna near by (now called Luni); it was consigned to special marble boats that sailed south to Ostia, the port of Rome, there to be lowered into barges and taken up the river to the city which it was transforming. The *marmo lunensis* was afterwards found as far away as England, in the Roman palace at Fishbourne in the second century AD, and centuries later in the tomb of Nelson, which had been made originally for Wolsey. Its uses, both artistic and practical, can be traced through the centuries. In our own day, for example, the sculptor Henry

---

[1] (In honour of William Walton, who, to the benefit of the community, developed the Carrara commerce, the Town Council in recognition erected this perpetual record in the year 1873.)

Moore chooses the purest marble, prised, not without danger, from the top of a mountain in Tuscany above Seravezza. And Queen Victoria, God bless her, on her monument in front of Buckingham Palace in London is sitting on a replica of the *Ara Pacis*, the Altar of Peace, erected in Rome by the Emperor Augustus, fashioned from no less than 1,000 tons of Carrara marble.

In summer there are daily tours of the quarries and the marble mountains starting from the coastal resorts, from Viareggio northwards; on a clear day the view from the mountains is breathtaking. A visit to a marble yard above Carrara gives one the impression that the stone itself has a strange, almost life-like quality. *'Il marmo e cattivo!'* remarks, with unexpected feeling, the foreman supervising the loading of marble slabs, steering us away from the swaying lorry on to which the slabs are being guided, bending its sides and breaking its wooden-slatted guard rails, and which looks as though it may turn over and deposit its load on us. To this man the marble is alive, it is 'nasty', is 'wicked'.

Among the many British who settled in or near Carrara in the nineteenth century because of the marble trade, three men are particularly interesting. They were very different from the spoiled young offspring of the nobility, completing their education on the Grand Tour, who passed through Florence and Siena. These were purposeful men of between twenty-five and thirty-five who had their living to earn, and had no especial interest in the culture of Tuscany. In each case they were held there by a fascination with the country, the people, and the marble.

The first was a young Scot from Leith, the port of Edinburgh, who had to carry on the family marble business when his father died. When his younger brother William reached the age of twenty, Alexander Thomson, known in his family as 'Sandie', decided to leave the business in his charge and go to Carrara to investigate the marble trade. He left Scotland on 15 August 1825, stopped in London to brief himself about the trade, and travelled to Leghorn.

With the ending of the Napoleonic Wars in 1814, Leghorn

had become a free port (and remained so until 1867), and the conditions of maritime trade were very favourable to foreigners. Alexander Thomson was clearly excited at the prospect of the purchase and export of Carrara marble, via Leghorn, to Leith and to London.

He wrote fully but with typical Scottish caution to his brother William, warning him not to imagine 'I have found some hidden treasure here, and that a fortune is to be made all at once'. He had come at a bad time, he reported, when there was a temporary inflation of marble prices, caused by 'the late rage for building in England', and particularly because of a 'Mr Brown from London'. (This was undoubtedly Joseph Browne, who was buying up marble on behalf of the architect John Nash, for the building he was doing for the Prince Regent.[2]) Because of the boom he was finding difficulty in locating good blocks of marble in the quarries, and because of inflationary prices he had to be cautious, buying only a few blocks to keep the business in Leith going.

He is avid for news from home, and for advice from William on how much of the first cargo he had consigned should be sold in London, and how much was required in Leith. Apparently he does not trust the 'London marble cutters'. But marble cutters must be laid off at Thomsons' own works, during the present slack period. 'The masons in the upper shop are all old hands and generally faithful, I would not like to part with any of them,' Alexander writes, adding that he would prefer, when it became necessary, to part with 'the labourers who cannot work advantageously by candlelight'.

The firm, however, was obviously thriving, for the family was moving to a bigger house:

You will perhaps find James Place a little inconvenient [wrote Alexander] as to the distance from work, but if you dine at four or five o'clock instead of two you will still be much at your ease . . . with the long telescope you will see the marble coming up the Firth while you sit over your glass of toddy.[3]

---

[2] J. Mordaunt Crook, *The History of the King's Works*, vol. VI (HMSO, 1973).
[3] Unpublished letters of Alexander Thomson, with Preface by Lt. Col. Kenneth Henderson, DSO. (Subsequent quotations in this chapter are from the same source.)

He was convinced they would be successful with a three-way business between London, Leith and Leghorn, with William loading the ships outwards from Leith, most probably with Scottish hard coal or 'splint', suitable for the furnaces of Tuscany where there was iron ore in plenty but no coal whatsoever.

Alexander prolonged his stay in Italy, ostensibly to study the language and the methods of commerce, but obviously also because he was enjoying himself. On 12 April 1826, he wrote to his brother from Leghorn that the change of climate was making him indolent, and he only wanted to 'lounge at a Window, smoke cigars and look at the ladies'. The weather was lovely and he was feeling very well. Then he gives William a little sermon on not listening to gossip and criticism that he, Sandie, was away from home so long. From his lofty age of thirty he speaks of a wisdom acquired in ignoring censure provided one is doing no harm to anyone else in the pursuit of pleasing oneself. Then he goes on to describe his life in Leghorn. He has subscribed to an 'extensive library' where he sees English and French newspapers and Edinburgh quarterly reviews, and he is assured such a privilege could not be found outside Tuscany. He now uses the Italian form of his signature, 'Alessandro Thomson'.

The British colony in Leghorn was large, able to maintain two churches, one Anglican, the other the Free Church of Scotland; and a British cemetery inside the walls became so overcrowded that another had to be opened outside in 1839. At some point Alexander confessed he had been so long in Leghorn he felt it was like home. If the business prospered he would need to fix a headquarters, and he would be happy there if he had enough to do; just now he felt at a loss after shipping the marble. His comment, 'England is going to the Devil', makes us laugh a century and a half later. Meanwhile he intended to make a little tour of Italy.

In June he went to Florence and from there wrote to his friend Thomas Henderson on 11 July 1826—glad, he says, that Thomas is so happy at Leghorn among 'all the pretty ladies of our acquaintance'. In answer to a query as to how he is standing the heat he admits to having 'long since relinquished the flannels' and to sleeping without a shirt; he still retains the nightcap, but without strapping it under the chin. He jokes that he is often without it in the morning, and blames 'the girl who sleeps in the next room for tearing it off'. In Florence he always walks in the shade so admirably afforded by the buildings. Unlike modern visitors he prefers Florence to the country during the hot months, and therefore proposes going to Bagni di Lucca only at the end of August when the fashionable season is over, and when, he hopes, the 'gaieties' there will be cheaper.

Though Alexander regarded the inhabitants of Carrara as 'peculiar people gather'd together from all parts of the world to search for good marble', Tuscans generally he found a peaceful, happy and hospitable people: 'They enjoy the riches that nature has bestowed upon them and they never torment their poor souls by thinking and reasoning and labouring like the English.' He declares, from Florence, that he has not heard of a suicide, a robbery or theft or any capital crime since he left Leghorn. Moreover Tuscany is very cheap:

> excellent coffee, toast & butter for 2½*d*, soup, bread, beef either roast or boil'd, vegetables of various sorts with vinegar and oil— delicious wine and a basket of fruit consisting of figs, pears, peaches, plums &c all for little more than one shilling.

For entertainment the pit in the chief theatre cost only 5*d* (three times as much for special performances). 'In fact I could live like a Gentleman, have a little palace of my own and keep my carriages and man servant all for £150 sterling a year.' And the young ladies of Tuscany are 'so loving and so kind and so yielding . . .'

From Florence he visited Pisa, where the feast of its patron saint, San Ranieri, celebrated only once every three or four years, happened to be in progress. People came hundreds of miles for this *festa*, when, Alexander reported, waxing eloquent,

> Temples were erected artificially on the Banks of the River—the Bridges were clad in fire—the Arno itself seemed a living stream of melted silver and the Palaces of the Princes studded with shining wax lights were seen reflected in his bosom . . . the sky was clear and serene, the Moon shone brighter than usual—she was jealous of this earthly blaze . . .

He was unimpressed by the horse and boat racing, however, and in general found the city dull, *una città morta*, he said. But during the feast the '*beau monde* of Florence and Lucca . . . half of Leghorn and the gentry from the surrounding country' made it gay.

In Florence he declared the Feast of San Giovanni was, except for the illuminations, 'more pompous still'. But he seems to have remained there, instead of going to Bagni di Lucca, until on 27 November he was back in Leghorn awaiting a steamer to Naples to make his way home.

After Alexander's return to Scotland the Thomsons struggled on with the business despite a lack of success in selling their marble through agents in London; they had to do their own selling. But the Greek–Gothic vogue in architecture was spreading and marble halls and fireplaces were status symbols. By 1835 Alexander had rented a house in Glasgow with an entrance hall large enough to make an impressive showroom for the firm's more elegant pieces of marble.

By 1839 the brothers had raised the money to finance the building, at Limekilns in Fife, of their own barque *Carrara*:

> She was a tubby little thing, only 88 feet long, and so broad in the beam that her registered tonnage was 218. She was very much a small, short-voyage craft—for her period, with a single deck, a short poop, a square stern and female figurehead.[4]

The female figurehead was the symbol of a superior merchant vessel. The *Carrara* was the first of a Thomson fleet of ships, for once they owned her their fortunes changed. They found themselves making a 'bonny penny' not through trafficking in marble as planned, but through using their ships for all kinds of marine business. They became founders of the Ben Line. The *Carrara* continued on the regular Leith–Leghorn run under a Captain Miller, but apparently, despite his early longings, Alexander did not follow her, but stayed behind in Scotland, to marry and grow rich.

[4] George Blake, *The Ben Line* (1956).

Twenty years after Alexander Thomson had given up his trade in Carrara marble, W. P. Jervis, Fellow of the Geographical Society, published a study of Italian mineral resources in which, having talked of the problem of processing the marble taken from the Apuan Alps into slabs, he concludes that:

> Of all the mills at Carrara, that of Mr Walton, the British Consul, bears the palm; he has erected a spacious building for twelve sawing frames, of which only six are yet erected. Each of these frames receives its motion by a connecting rod attached to a drum revolving with the main shaft running along the whole length of the building, and furnished with a fly wheel. . . . A travelling crane moves on a railway placed under the roof in the direction of the building, and serves for loading or unloading the blocks from the ox waggons. . . .
>
> Mr Walton does not employ a vertical wheel, like the other gentlemen, but a turbine of about 50 horse-power, which sets in motion the main shaft. The fall of the water is not very great, but the mill stream is a powerful one.[5]

This William Walton, who dominated the Carrara marble business of the nineteenth century, modernized it, and built up the trade with England and America particularly, was a Yorkshireman. Born in 1796, he emigrated to Seravezza in or about 1830, after the early death of his wife, and bought a marble firm from an Englishman named Beresford.

Walton was energetic, and had an eye on the future. While building a road to transport the marble from the mountains of Levigliani to the sea, he was managing the Bardiglio–Fiorito quarries at Monalto and Retignano, and appears also to have erected one of the first mechanized sawmills in the area, near Ruosina, and another machine for sanding marble slabs near Monte Costa.

In 1840 he moved to Carrara, and was one of the first to introduce marble-working machinery there. Walton became a person of influence in Carrara, later (1855–65) acting as American as well as Honorary British Consul there, and over the next quarter of

---

[5] W. P. Jervis, *Mineral Resources of Central Italy* (1862).

a century he was able to put the American marble trade, as well
as the British, on its feet. In 1844 Charles Dickens and his wife
broke their journey south from Genoa to stay with Walton at
Carrara. Later, in *Pictures from Italy*, Dickens gave a vivid account
of the marble quarries of those days.

> so many openings, high up in the hills, on either side of these
> passes, where they blast and excavate for marble; which may turn
> out good or bad: may make a man's fortune very quickly, or ruin
> him by the great expense of working what is worth nothing. Some
> of these caves were opened by the ancient Romans, and remain as
> they left them to this hour. Many others are being worked at this
> moment; others are to be begun tomorrow, next week, next
> month; others are unbought, unthought of; and marble enough
> for more ages than have passed since the place was resorted to, lies
> hidden everywhere; patiently awaiting its time of discovery.

The novelist described the process of bringing the marble
down from the mountains, in carts 'drawn, as they used to be,
five hundred years ago, by oxen' and expostulated over the
cruelty both to animals and men:

> Two pairs, four pair, ten pair, twenty pair, to one block, according
> to its size; down it must come, this way. In their struggling from
> stone to stone, with their enormous loads behind them, they die
> frequently upon the spot; and not they alone; for their passionate
> drivers, sometimes tumbling down in their energy, are crushed to
> death beneath the wheels.

He watched a driver goading a pair of oxen through a stream:

> He had a great rod in his hand with an iron point: and when they
> could plough and force their way through the loose bed of the
> torrent no longer, and came to a stop, he poked it into their bodies,
> beat it on their heads, screwed it round and round in their nostrils,
> got them on a yard or two, in the madness of intense pain;
> repeated all these persuasions with increased intensity of purpose,
> when they stopped again . . .

and later reflected:

Standing in one of the many studios of Carrara that afternoon—
for it is a great workshop, full of beautifully-furnished copies in
marble, of almost every figure, group, and bust, we know—it
seemed at first, so strange to me that those exquisite shapes, replete
with grace, and thought, and delicate repose, should grow out of
all this toil, and sweat and torture! . . .[6]

Italy's revolution of 1848 brought the marble business almost
to a standstill, but Walton persuaded his foreign contacts to
continue investing against the return of peaceful times. By 1851
he was overseeing the construction of the first loading pier at
Marina di Carrara, known to this day as Walton's pier; 280
metres long, it revolutionized the loading process, until then
done manually from oxen-driven vehicles on the sands. (Since
Walton's, three piers in all were built at the Marina di Carrara,
and in 1877 a fourth, not now used, at Forte dei Marmi.) In 1854
he headed a committee for the construction of a railway, the
Ferrovia Marmifera, and between 1853 and 1857, overcoming
immense difficulties, he built two large modern sawmills with
twenty-two frames driven by water power, supplemented by
steam, in addition to a number of sanding beds.

Between 1837 and 1846 2,258 people were employed in the
marble trade, and Walton told Jervis in 1862 that about £6,000
was paid weekly at Carrara to 'artists, sculptors, quarrymen,
boatmen and drivers . . . a sum not less than £300,000 per
annum'. About half the marble blocks were exported to the
United States, which was a steady market until the outbreak of
the Civil War; of the balance one-third went to Britain and two-
thirds to the rest of Europe.

The strong-minded William Walton loved Carrara, and
when, on 20 July 1857, he had to report to his diplomatic
superior, the Marquis of Normandy, that 'on the night of the
15th inst some malicious persons defaced and destroyed blocks
to the value of two hundred pounds sterling', it gave him immense satisfaction to add that, 'from the appearance . . . the
people of Carrara feel indignant that after a residence of 25
years'[7] he should have been thus treated. Moreover he had, he

---

[6] *Pictures from Italy*, with an Introduction by David Paroissien (1973).
[7] Foreign Office, 170.81 (Public Record Office).

said, no intention of bringing a claim on the government of Modena or the people of Carrara, he only wanted a speedy discovery of the offender.

Even he grew weary, however, and his consular dispatch of 1865 revealed that he had been out of business for some time and wished to retire owing to age and health.[8] He returned to England and died at the place of his birth, Wakefield, in 1872. The following year the Commune of Carrara erected the memorial tablet in his honour.

Walton's business connections with his nephews the Gooddys of Liverpool, and later with Richard Cripps of Bristol, eventually resulted in the firm of Walton, Gooddy & Cripps, which had large marble yards in London, Liverpool and Bristol. It was they who supplied the marble for the monument to Queen Victoria in front of Buckingham Palace, completed in 1909.

The only member of the families in this firm still in the marble business in Carrara is Percy Greville Howard Cripps, a dynamic octogenarian, a slim spring-heeled man of six feet seven inches, with kindly blue eyes and a healthy colour. He arrived in Italy in 1920, and after spending several months in Siena learning the language, came to Carrara to help George Herbert Gibbs, then running the important 'marble worked' department of the firm. There was in Carrara at that time a large colony of British, who met daily at midday at a bar in the Piazza d'Armi.

After the First World War the principal firms in Carrara had had to equip the various quarries and yards with modern machinery, in order to meet the colossal flow of orders for marble. Much of this was for 'cemetery work', Victorian piety having set a fashion for marble gravestones and memorials. Also, in the early part of the century there were large orders from Britain for random-sized slabs and scantlings for use as fishmongers' slabs, butchers' counters, and fireplaces. But in the 1930s these firms were caught by a sudden severe slump. The Mussolini regime had added to the difficulties by creating a consortium, by which all marble went into a pool, to be distributed

8 ibid., 170.130.

as the Fascists thought fit. Naturally this did not work to the advantage of those not sympathetic to the regime, and many firms were ruined.

Major Cripps himself started from scratch three times in the trade, after economic recessions, and had his own troubles with the Fascists. Renata, the Carrara girl he married in 1931, was a refugee in England throughout the Second World War, while her family in Italy suffered near-starvation and were trapped in the Gothic Line as the Germans retreated north in 1944. The Apuan mountains were a stronghold of the partisans at this time, and when Allied prisoners-of-war managed to escape from their camps when the Italian government surrendered to the Allies, they were aided by villagers in the mountains, braving the certain retaliation of the Germans.

Greville Cripps is totally involved in the craft of marble and its commerce. He is proudly aware that Carrara white marble deposits are still considered the finest in the world: when Mussolini wanted a grandiose column for the stadium at Rome, to rival those of the Roman emperors, a block of some 300 tons was cut. There were difficulties in getting it to the port, and bridges had to be strengthened *en route*, but, as of old, it was taken by sea in a special barge, via Ostia and up the Tiber to Rome.

Large blocks can still be sent down from the quarries—there are strata of marble 2–3 metres thick, of unknown width, and where the strata run straight, columns like Mussolini's can be produced at will—but they are now limited in size and weight by the size of the frames for sawing, and the lifting capacity of the various cranes—a maximum of about fifty tons. The saw frames are limited in size because, however long the blade, and however taut, excessive length would produce a wobble in the powered sawing, causing unevenness in the slab. In recent years diamond saw frames,[9] some with a dozen or so blades, have been installed, which cut the marble with great speed and precision, but the cost of these is enormous.

Since today many people choose to be cremated, and there is the added problem of the upkeep of churchyards, the cemetery

---

[9] Invented by the French engineer Jacquin.

trade in marble has languished. Also the uses of marble are changing: Major Cripps recently received an enquiry for 2,000 tons of the finest white marble powder for toothpaste! Swimming pools are now lined with marble dust, and black and white tiles for flooring are also in great demand.

There have been changes, too, in the handling and transporting of the marble. The lorries nowadays come right up to the quarry, whereas not so long ago (after the day of the oxen was over) the blocks were put on *lizze* (literally 'slides') to be propelled, guided, and slid down the steep road. Today blocks of twenty to twenty-five tons are loaded by a relatively small motorized crane, then tied securely and balanced in the centre of the truck, to be taken to the marble yards below. And once the blocks are cut and ready, in the yards, a container will be put on a lorry for La Spezia, then loaded on to a ship for England, or sent by road direct through Switzerland and France, and across the Channel to Felixstowe or one of the other ports specializing in container traffic. Ideally, by these means, an order could be in England in three days; in actual fact it takes two to three weeks to deliver a consignment.

Now eighty-five, Greville Cripps is semi-retired at Carrara, but is still active, walking to fetch an English and an Italian newspaper every day, and fishing in the Appenines in the summer. As recently as seven years ago he enjoyed the walk to the quarries, starting at 6 a.m. and taking two hours, joining in the singing of the men on the way and having breakfast on arrival. But now most of the workers hurry to work and back to their homes by car or motor scooter.

On one of our visits to Carrara, Major Cripps arranged for us to go up to see the Lorano quarry, one of a group of quarries being leased by the workers and the highest in use at the time. At first we travel up a very good tarmac road, but nearing the quarry we turn off and go round sharp zig-zag curves which the lorries have to negotiate, coming down to the yards below with their heavy blocks of marble. We leave the car and climb the last part on foot, up steps cut into the blocks of marble, between steep banks consisting of pieces of marble arranged one on top of another, covered by close-meshed wire to prevent slips.

From a platform immediately below the site of the actual

quarrying, we can see the huge circular diamond saw, which can cut through a block of marble in less than a minute, while near by the more old-fashioned sawing frame works steadily with water and sand, taking about ten minutes to get through the same size of block. We then climb to the final ledge where the marble is cut from the mountain by the usual method of wire ropes, sand and water. One of the wire ropes which cuts through the marble has broken off and lashed into the air, and it is easy to see how it could whip off the head of a worker. Higher up the mountain we watch a large modern digger pushing enormous mounds of broken marble pieces over the cliff face of the platform on which a team of men is working. One of them balances unsteadily on the broken pieces, and it is not difficult to imagine he might go over the edge.

The perils of marble quarrying and processing were made vivid for us by this visit. Yet the marble has a fascination for those who work with it, whether in the quarries or the workshops; this beautiful stone is regarded almost as a living creature. The workmen are pitting their strength, their skill and their brains against it. Although every year, despite all modern precautions and regulations, there are serious accidents in the quarries and in the yards, these men are not deterred by the danger, for their lives, like those of the many generations of their families before them, are devoted to conquering the beautiful and the wicked marble.

·☾ XII ☽·

A British Prisoner-of-war in Florence:
General Sir Richard O'Connor,
KT GCB CB DSO

LIFE in a charming eighteenth-century grand duchy is a big step away from tank warfare in the desert in our own time, but that step takes us to one of the strongest links in the Tuscan connection with England. General Sir Richard O'Connor[1] is a lover of Italy and of Tuscany especially, and he has good reason to be.

I met the General soon after the war, through the historian Sir Arthur Bryant, and thirty years later, in 1979, I found myself seated beside him at a luncheon to celebrate Sir Arthur's eightieth birthday. It was hard, on that second occasion, to realize that Sir Richard himself was approaching his ninetieth birthday. He is a small, compact man with an open, attractive face and personality; apart from deafness in one ear, time has dealt kindly with him since his years as a prisoner-of-war in Italy, 1941 to 1944. His intense application to physical fitness and his irrepressible energy were invaluable in those frustrating years of escape attempts that failed, and periods of solitary confinement followed by more escape planning. He told me that he could not have gone on, during detention, if he had not concentrated totally on the possibility of escape.

He was a tank and armoured warfare specialist; he had been the right-hand man of Wavell in the first swift North African campaign, and obviously would have figured prominently in later campaigns if he had not been taken prisoner. He and

---

[1] I greatly regret to report that General O'Connor died not long after this was written.

164

General Philip Neame, VC, fell into German hands near Derna in April 1941. Somewhat to O'Connor's relief, they were handed over to the Italians, whom he had always liked, having fought alongside them in the First World War when he was a colonel in command of a battalion. The two generals and members of their staff who had happened to be with them when captured, including Brigadier J. Combe, were sent to a prison camp at Sulmona in the Abruzzi. Here the Italian commandant allowed a junior officer from a near-by camp, who had been taken prisoner during a British commando raid in Sicily, to visit them. In the short time available he was able to teach the other officers a code which they used throughout their captivity.

In September 1941 they were moved to Florence, to the Castello Vincigliato above Fiesole, with towers and high stone battlements, and a sentry walk all round the inside. The castle dated from A.D. 1031 or earlier, but had been almost completely rebuilt between 1855 and 1865 by an English Liberal M.P., John Temple Leader, who remained in Tuscany and made his home in the fortress. General Sir Adrian Carton de Wiart, who had lost both an arm and an eye in North Africa, and who was described by Churchill as 'a model of chivalry and honour', described their arrival:

We had been told that Vincigliata was at Fiesole; the Italians breathed the name with such enchantment that I could well picture all the charms of the *Decameron* and was only wondering what we should do by day. . . . I do know that Queen Victoria lunched there . . . and I know better still that I thought it was the most horrible-looking place I had ever seen. It was a fortress . . . surrounded by ramparts and high walls, bristling with sentries all armed to the teeth. Our hearts . . . sank within us. . . .

We were in a small way consoled by the aspect of our new Commandant, the Duke of Montalto, who had been educated at Cheltenham, spoke perfect English and seemed to understand the British outlook and mentality.[2]

Though Mussolini had finally joined Hitler in the war, many

[2] Lt.Gen. Sir Adrian Carton de Wiart, VC KBE CB CMG DSO, *Happy Odyssey* (1950).

Italians had kept their feelings of friendship for their one-time allies, the British. In fact, the British officers were at first well treated at Vincigliata; and according to Philip Neame, Montalto was removed as commandant because he became too friendly with his prisoners, finally having accepted their invitation to dinner on Christmas Day![3] The prison medical officer, Dr Bolaffio, who had a practice in Florence, was also pro-English and anti-Fascist, and lent the officers maps and guidebooks to help in their escape plans. He too was sent away. A sergeant major, Ficozzi, owner of a shop in Florence patronized by the British, would purchase food and wine for them, but he took great care not to be observed by the *carabinieri* who were in charge of them. Even their batmen were allowed to be with them until an escape plot was uncovered in April 1943.

From December 1942 they were receiving coded messages from the War Office with information and advice about escaping, and later were sent books and games in which money and maps were concealed. It was made clear that it was a duty to try to escape, but naturally some were keener than others, and the penalties that would be inflicted on those who stayed behind after a breakout had to be considered. However, O'Connor and Carton de Wiart and two others had decided previously to try to get to the French frontier, and to this end collected food and clothing and rucksacks. At the same time they began rigorous training, carrying packs up and down stairs and rope-climbing. A new white-washed brick wall, ten feet high, had been built to separate them from the Italian guard quarters, and here, in the early hours of the morning, they found they could practise in privacy.

They did, indeed, have a good deal of freedom from observation. But this first escape attempt, in April 1942, which involved a climb over the white wall, failed, and the sentries were afterwards more alert. Some of the prisoners' kit and food and papers was found and confiscated, and from then on there was a check once each night by an Italian officer. Their parcels were more carefully examined and, as General O'Connor reported afterwards, 'we were spoken to severely by the Commander of the

[3] Lt.Gen. Sir Philip Neame, VC, *Playing with Strife* (1947).

Florence *Difese*, General Chiappi, who nevertheless proved to be an Italian of the best type.'[4]

Outside lighting was greatly augmented so that it seemed better to try an escape by day, and O'Connor decided to undertake this alone. As the Italian commandant had thought such an attempt impossible, the day sentries had been reduced in order to increase the night guard, but the positions and movements of the sentries at all times had to be worked out. Another problem was that a rope would have to be anchored to a position on the walls where there had originally been loopholes. Some of these had been filled with flower boxes, but one of them was empty, and it was thought possible to make a block of wood with one end the same shape and size as the flower boxes, paint in red the end that could be seen, and fix a hook on the outside end of the block sufficiently strong to bear the weight of General O'Connor. He would have to push the block into the aperture, fix the rope to the hook, and slide down it. He would be wearing civilian clothes underneath his uniform which, just before being hoisted on to the wall, he would stow under the stone bench from which he would be hoisted.

Sheets were used to make 49 feet of rope, in 7-foot lengths (though it was thought only 28 feet would be used), and daily practice sessions began in O'Connor's room. Two assistants would hoist the General to the top of the wardrobe, as they would have to do on the wall, whilst he bore his valise and got the rope and the block into place. (From the twinkle in O'Connor's eye, as he described this phase to me, I should guess the two assistants got some fun watching his struggles!) Eventually he became expert enough to make the ascent in a few seconds.

When the day of the attempt arrived he sauntered out to the stone bench in the courtyard. Valise, rope and block had been hidden under the bench in advance, behind buckets of earth for the plants. O'Connor had just time, between the passing of one sentry and another, to strip down to the plain clothes he wore under his uniform. At the signal he was hoisted up as they had

---

[4] General O'Connor's report in the King's College Military Archive, from which further quotations in this account are taken.

practised, but the wall to his dismay was higher than the wardrobe had been. As he gave a kick to get all the way up, the block of wood must have turned and the rope became twisted round the hook, so that he lost at least five vital seconds untangling it. But he slid down the rope and had almost reached the ground when he heard a shout and saw the sentry leaning out of the embrasure with his rifle pointed at him, not more than 15 yards away!

O'Connor decided that even if the sentry missed at that range, he could never get down to the Florence railway station, so he waited quietly to be recaptured. He managed to throw his money and maps back over the white wall, where they were recovered, unseen, by his companions, before he was taken to the headquarters of the *carabinieri*. The Commandant became near-hysterical and abused the sentry for letting O'Connor get on to the wall and for not firing. He reported to higher command that the prisoner had given his parole not to try to escape, but O'Connor wrote to General Chiappi at Florence headquarters, who at once accepted his word, for he knew that the British did not give their parole.

The other Italian officers and many of the NCOs and *carabinieri* 'were very nice' to him and tried to shake his hand in congratulation. Although there were severe penalties for any act of friendship towards the British, General Chiappi came up later and gave the sentry in question 500 lire for not firing, for acting in a sensible manner and keeping his head.

O'Connor's punishment was solitary confinement for the month of September 1942 'in a fortress' in the region of Genoa. The cell had only two tiny windows, high up, and the electric light was not strong enough to read by at night. He had a bed, table, chair, washstand and two chamber pots. Two hours' exercise was allowed daily on the battlements. Food was sent from the main camp with which he was not allowed to communicate, but he 'managed to carry on quite a satisfactory correspondence by writing on the inside of the lid of my mess tin'. He took a great deal of exercise and remained fit. According to Carton de Wiart, whilst in solitary confinement O'Connor studied and perfected his Italian, which he would need for any journey after the breakout that was already in his mind. When the sentence had been served, he was escorted back to Vincigliata, as he had been on the way out, by a colonel commanding an infantry regiment in Florence, a staff officer and two *carabinieri*. They treated him very well, O'Connor said, the staff officer having been awarded a British decoration, the MC, during the First World War when Italy had been our ally.

Meanwhile in Vincigliata, escape attempts having failed both by night and by day, his friends had decided to tunnel under the perimeter wall. At dawn, before the Italians were up, they explored the well-shaft, from which, they had learned, in mediaeval fortresses an underground passage often led to the outside. One such passage was indeed found and they inched along it to a small cellar and in the opposite direction as far as a bricked-up wall. It seemed possible to drive a tunnel from that cellar under the courtyard of the castle and the entrance drive, then under the outside wall, to freedom. It would be 90 to 100 feet long. But General Neame, who was a sapper and had done some tunnelling in the First World War, decided it was an impossible task with the poor tools at their disposal.

They immediately began to devise an alternative plan, based on their study of a book on the history of the castle which they had discovered among the furniture in a closed room. Next to the big dining room was the chapel, behind a sealed-up door with a high grille over it. They found they could get into the chapel via the shaft for the service lift which was used to bring up their food. They achieved this by breaking through a wall consisting of two foot six inches of masonry, working at 'safe' periods of the day, between 7.30 and 9.30 a.m. and between 2 and 4 p.m., and making as little noise as possible with their improvised tools: short iron crowbars, a carpenter's chisel and mallet, and a bricklayer's trowel.

The chapel, as they saw when they got through to it, and a lobby which led into it, were both full of stored furniture and carpets. Neame devised a scheme of sinking a shaft in the lobby, which meant they would only have to tunnel under the court-yard wall and not under the keep wall, with its deeper founda-tions. Air Marshal Boyd, a skilled carpenter, was put in charge of the working party, with watchers in the upstairs room, and messengers detailed from the remainder of the party.

At this point O'Connor returned from solitary confinement and joined the escape party. He then took charge of the working party, Carton de Wiart of the watching party, and Neame was chairman and chief engineer. Neame worked out 'dimensions, slope and lengths of shaft and tunnel'. The first shaft was made 10 feet deep, with an opening 4 feet by 2, running across and under the driveway to the outer wall. They got right under the courtyard wall, and drove the tunnel down a slope of 1 in 8 so as to be fourteen feet deep when they reached the massive outer wall. The problem of emergence and concealment had then to be carefully considered. Neame inspected the tunnel regularly wearing his white pyjamas over his clothes; these could be discarded if there was an alarm, and he would not be caught with dirty clothes. The soil was very difficult to work, as it was hardened clay with frequent horizontal strata of hard rock which split into blocks. Work was halted by a bell whenever a sentry above approached within ten yards. Lacking explosives or miners' tools, five inches a day was, therefore, reasonable progress.

On the last lap a layer of rock lying above the shaft near the surface proved such a hazard that it almost ruined the project. But they pressed on doggedly until only six to nine inches of earth remained. A lid, camouflaged with paint and pine needles, successfully hid their exit hole. It had taken them six months, from September 1942 to March 1943, to complete a 16-foot shaft down, a 35-foot tunnel sloping downwards and a rising shaft of 7 feet. All of the earth was laboriously dragged back along the tunnel to the chapel, and they worked in near-airless conditions.

It was decided that six officers should escape as soon as it was dark, since the night check by the guards was not made until between 1 a.m. and 3 a.m. Dummy bodies were made up by the batmen, with real hair, which were so convincing that a guard later declared he had heard one of them say 'Goodnight'. Over the months food and clothing had been carefully collected by various means, and this, together with money, maps and compasses, was distributed amongst the six escapees. They were to

disperse in pairs: Miles and Hargest, both New Zealand briga-
diers; Combe and Air Marshal Boyd; and lastly O'Connor and
Carton de Wiart—the latter immensely grateful to be included
since, lacking an arm and an eye, he had not been able to do any
tunnelling, and was also difficult to disguise.

A rainy night was chosen, when the guards stayed in their
sentry boxes. The six officers changed clothes and assembled in
the dining room, then proceeded with their baggage through
the tunnel. Their colleagues had already opened the exit lid, and
they then moved silently through the trees to a gateway, fortunately unfastened, in the outer garden leading to the road.
Miles and Hargest, and Combe and Boyd, walked straight down
to the Florence railway station, whilst O'Connor and Carton de
Wiart started their long march across the Apennines to
Switzerland.

Carrying heavy rucksacks of food, they walked across country
through beautiful mountain scenery. Carton de Wiart tells how
he suffered acutely from an inflamed toe, blaming himself for
not having taken sufficient walking practice before the escape.
At night they slept in warm cowsheds offered by friendly
farmers, with whom they posed as Austrian tourists on a walking
tour. One night they were forced to take shelter under a farm
cart in a farmyard. They had covered 150 miles in seven days'
walking, O'Connor doing the map reading, and their forged
passes had been accepted twice, before a police patrol on bicycles
stopped and questioned them. It was obvious that they were the
missing prisoners for whom a search was in progress, and their
period of freedom was abruptly ended.

When they returned to Vincigliata they were given thirty
days' solitary confinement in their rooms. This was by no means
displeasing to them; obviously they were not sent away because
the authorities had no wish to draw attention to the escapes.
Meanwhile Miles and Hargest had escaped by train to Switzerland, but Boyd and Combe, who got separated, failed in their
train exploits. They too were returned to the castle, where an
enormous row had blown up after the discovery of the escape:
the garrison was increased to some one hundred and fifty infantry and *carabinieri*, to guard eleven British officers and fourteen other ranks.

★   ★   ★

During the summer of '43 Carton de Wiart was taken off to Rome, and eventually to Lisbon, to assist in negotiating the terms of the Italian surrender, presumably because he was a friend of the Italian royal family. He told O'Connor afterwards that he had been unable to make the terms, which were those of unconditional surrender, less harsh for the Italians. Afterwards, though he offered to return to Vincigliata, the Italians set him free and he returned to England.

On 7 September 1943 the Commandant of the castle announced to the prisoners assembled in the drawing room that an armistice had been signed between the Allies and Italy. For the moment General Chiappi, in charge of the Florence area, thought it better for them to remain in Vincigliata; he would let them know as soon as possible what they should do. The Italian sentries remained on duty next day and O'Connor took the opportunity to reward the sentry who had refrained from firing on him during his attempted escape over the wall. A day later they were taken to General Chiappi's headquarters in Florence, after changing into whatever civilian clothes they had, and packing their belongings in suitcases. A telephone call to the General had brought the news that the Germans were making for Florence, and he at once sent the prisoners off to the station in a lorry, advising them to go by the first train to Arezzo, to keep out of the way of the Germans.

He himself, General Armellini Chiappi, was not able to keep out of the Germans' way. He was sixty-four in 1943, an age at which a man might be expected to be 'sensible'. But he had been a soldier all his active life, and true to his ingrained traditions (and personal feelings), he refused to collaborate with the German Army. He was sent to a prisoner-of-war camp at Wollstein in Poland where, as I learned from Italian Army headquarters in Rome, he died in November 1944. He was given a posthumous award for valour, for refusing repeated German offers of release provided he cooperated with them, when, away from camp conditions, he might have recovered his health.

Meanwhile the British prisoners General Chiappi had released had reached the station at Florence. There they found a number of friendly Italians ready to exchange clothes with them, having a preference for British leather footwear which they said was of better quality than their own. General Neame says the prisoners could have passed for 'seedy-looking Italians and greasily garbed railway workers' when they boarded the train for Arezzo. On arrival they were taken to the mess of the Italian Officers' School, where they felt they were not particularly welcome. The Italians knew as little as the released prisoners of the military situation. To them suddenly the British had become allies, yet they feared German retaliation.

According to General Neame it was the head of the Arezzo police who came to their rescue. He provided two buses driven by plain-clothes policemen which took them forty miles north to a monastery in the Apennines called Camaldoli, partly a foundation of the Dominican Order and partly a tourist centre. Here they stayed for four days, after which, as people were becoming curious, it was decided to move them to villages further up in the mountains. The four senior British officers went to Eremo, a thousand feet higher up, where the Prior General of the Camaldolese order lived. This was a large monastery with friendly priests of various nationalities. So far the Germans had not visited them, but they had installed an underground telephone wire from the monastery at Camaldoli, so as to have warning of their approach.

At Eremo each officer was given a small, simple cubicle and adequate food. They had left their belongings hidden behind the high altar at Camaldoli and these were later moved up and hidden in the roof of the fifteenth-century monastery library. When, later, the Germans came, the Prior General had their things hidden more securely, in an empty stone-built tomb in the chapel cemetery, which was then sealed up and a false name and date inscribed. Don Leoni, one of the brothers, was detailed to act as liaison with the prisoners. He was a fair-skinned Italian who rode about the mountains in his long white robe on a mule with a flask of *vino bianco* hanging from the saddle. During this period O'Connor and a companion did a night reconnaissance of the main road, and from a hideout observed long convoys of German lorries driving north with furniture and other loot.

The Prior General eventually arranged for the senior officers to go to an isolated hamlet called Seghetina, high up in the Apennines, and paid for their keep. Eight officers lived there and thirty or more other ranks were scattered around in peasants' cottages. Conditions were primitive, naturally, with a bed of straw or a mattress in an attic, two to a bed and no modern sanitation. All the men helped the peasants with their work of cultivating the soil, fetching water from the bottom of the gorge, and husking maize. Their diet consisted mainly of pasta, polenta, rice and minestrone. Once or twice a week Neame and O'Connor climbed up and down and round the mountain to keep in contact with the other prisoners. They felt entirely secure as there were no roads to the hamlet which would take a car, although the possibility of a German approach by night from the main road over the gully had to be considered.

The peasants at Seghetina were anti-Fascist. Their leader, Lorenzo Rossi, was a tall, handsome young man, a tireless worker, who had evaded military service by deliberately having all his teeth pulled out. After some days a discussion about security resulted in Rossi's having two brushwood huts built in the forest, about a mile from the village, where the officers could all sleep, returning to the village each morning. They had been perhaps ten days in the mountain hamlet when a young Italian, Bruno Vailati, arrived, saying he wished them to meet the local political leaders. He was obviously highly placed in the partisan organization, for he offered to get a message to General Alexander through the enemy lines.

Several leaders of the Union of Italian Labour then visited them. First came Signor Nanni, a lawyer who owned a printing works; he had quarrelled with Mussolini over his imperialist ideas, and had been exiled at one period. But Spada (whose name, meaning 'sword', may have been assumed) was the man who impressed Neame most. Of peasant origin, he had proved himself a natural leader, of high ideals and integrity. His aim was to help guide Italy away from the 'graft, corruption and false ideas of Fascism'. Though the death penalty was now in force for any Italian helping an escaped prisoner-of-war, these men, undaunted, continued to give the British officers and men money, clothes, boots and food.

One morning when Neame and O'Connor were making their

usual reconnaissance before entering the village, they spotted Germans surrounding some of the cottages. They decided to vacate the brushwood shelter and go deeper into the forest. Heavy rain made the stream they usually crossed to get to the village impassable; it also discouraged the Germans. Unaware of this, Neame and O'Connor moved on until, soaked and cold, they found shelter for the night in a cattle shed where the only way to avoid being asphyxiated by the fire they lit was to lie flat and let the smoke rise. Lorenzo Rossi brought a box of food, which, considering how short the villagers were themselves, was extremely generous. He reported that the Germans had bullied the villagers, but no one would betray the British. Rossi thought, however, that the villagers were now frightened, and that the officers should move to a village called Straubatenze, some five or six miles away, and contact the miller there.

On 30 October O'Connor, Combe, Ranfurly and Neame set off on a five-hour march across the mountains to Straubatenze, where they found shelter on the farm of some friendly Italians. Then, when morale was rather low, came a note from the Prior General at Eremo saying a British agent would rescue Generals O'Connor and Neame and Air Marshal Boyd, the three senior men in the party; they collected their belongings and climbed for two hours up a narrow goat track to meet the Italian guide sent by the British agent. Next day they had a twenty-mile march across the mountains to the monastery at La Verna, where a Signor Cognazzo met them with a motor car full of bicycles provided by Lieutenant Fergusson of the Royal Corps of Signals, the British agent in charge of their escape. For the next seven weeks Cognazzo, a resourceful and fearless man, devoted himself to working out their escape; when this was finally achieved it was happily possible for both him and his wife to be taken with them to safety.

O'Connor's bicycle happened to be a lady's but this did not deter him on their exciting three-day journey to the coast at Cattolica, where they hoped to be taken off by submarine. On the way their guide, who was riding ahead, pedalled back to warn them the Germans were preparing a bridge for demolition. He hoped that a path would be left for bicycles. The guide went first as arranged, and all went well. O'Connor was next and prepared to dismount when he arrived at the German demolition party but he was waved on, and the other two followed, vastly relieved to have got over in safety. At a farm house where they were given a meal, they heard for the first time the British news on the wireless, that the Allies were demanding unconditional surrender from both Germany and Italy. The Italians felt this would lengthen the war, and that they should have had milder treatment than the Germans.

In Cattolica the men stayed at a house that belonged to an Englishman who had so far managed to conceal his nationality. From there they made their first attempt to rendezvous with the submarine by row boat but no submarine arrived. Spada now re-entered their lives and took them off by bicycle to the state of San Marino, where they stayed for ten depressingly idle days, allowed to speak only to the local priest. Spada then rode off with them at five in the morning, going southwards along the coast, and they were lodged comfortably for the night in a village whose name they never knew. Next day they received forged identification papers; O'Connor's was signed by the Italian Command office. They stayed at Forli with an Italian lawyer, Utila, and left early for Signor Spazzoli's villa near Forli, where they stayed a week. This was a particularly brave family, whose two sons had created trouble for the Germans and were eventually killed in an affray. Spazzoli himself was later arrested, and tried by the Germans, then executed. After the war O'Connor went back to visit the family, thinking to find them justifiably bitter, but he was welcomed with open arms and they were proud to have helped the British.

The second attempt to contact a submarine which was scheduled to take them off also failed. Posing as Swiss refugees from the bombing of Ancona, they walked out of Cattolica with Spada, though they had begged him not to accompany them because if caught he would certainly be executed. Spada told them that since Fascism began twenty-five years before he had been perpetually in exile or in prison or in hiding for his political beliefs.

Italian friends, Sovera, Cognazzo and Spada, had been in touch with various partisan groups seeking their help, but noth-ing came of this; there was much rivalry between these groups, and sometimes even hostility. (At one point O'Connor was shown, by a communist, the arsenal of a partisan group which, it was explained, was for use not against the Germans but against the Italian government after the war.) After ten days they had to clear out of the chapel where they had been staying, by an arrangement made by Spada with the local priest. Spada and a friend arrived after dark with four bicycles despite the curfew. Finally, after being cared for by more Italians, they arrived again at Signor Spazzoli's villa in a suburb of Forli, where they lived comfortably for seven days, keeping the house completely shuttered by day.

Bruno Vailati, the young partisan leader they had met in the mountains while under the care of the monks, had meanwhile had adventures in getting through the German lines to the British Headquarters on their behalf. He arrived in Rome by train and cycled south to near Capua, from where he walked. The Germans arrested him but he pretended to be a local doctor, and having once been a medical student he was so convincing that the German officer drove him part of the way to visit a patient. Soon after this he was forced by a German tank crew to march in front of them with his hands up, down a village street. In a narrow part he dodged down a side street and escaped. In order to cross the German lines he had to hide by day and crawl into the American zone at night. He showed the Americans Neame's note addressed to Generals Alexander or Montgomery, and they passed him on to the British Army, where a plan of escape was worked out for the prisoners. Vailati then went up the coast in a fishing boat, landing in the area where, he was told, he would find the prisoners-of-war. After the war General Neame recommended Bruno Vailati for the Military Cross for his bravery and resourcefulness.

A fifth attempt was made to get the British officers off the coast on 23 November, but the rescue ship did not turn up. They were then placed in an empty villa in Cervia, and given food supplied by the near-by hotel owned by Signor Sovera, who, some time before, had been an under-manager at Claridge's Hotel in London, and who proved to be a wonderful friend. Again the Italians made exact arrangements for the taking off of the generals and again, on 24 November, the ship did not arrive.

Afterwards they were told that the visit of the British ships on these two occasions had to be cancelled owing to naval operations in the Adriatic.

They were eventually taken off by an Italian fishing vessel, whose captain had to be paid £800. This was supplied by Signor Arpesella on receipt of an IOU and an explanatory letter. The plan was for the vessel to sail into the harbour at Cattolica at dusk, just before the crews left their boats for the night. The officers would board in the dark and spend the night in the hold, battened down; in the morning the crew would start up their engines as usual. The captain had to decide with Signor Arpesella which would be the most favourable night; the latter would drive them to a point within walking distance of the harbour, where they would be guided to the boat.

The plan worked, but once aboard the vessel, the British officers became very anxious about the reliability of the captain; also the hold was stuffy and strongly smelling of fish. Fortunately the Germans did not make an inspection. As they moved out of the mouth of the harbour next morning they heard shouting. O'Connor feared that the harbour officials were remonstrating because the boat had not been inspected, but, according to Neame, the ship stopped and the captain handed over his papers. They then continued on their course, and bad weather and poor visibility made it difficult for the Germans on shore to see them. In the hold they were all very sick; O'Connor said he had never felt so ill. On the way the weather cleared and the moon came out. They were then allowed on deck, and about midnight changed course and travelled south where they could see the guns firing from both sides of the battle lines.

They were arrested by the British when they landed at Termoli. O'Connor asked to see the officer in charge and was astonished to find Professor Douglas Grant, who had been on O'Connor's staff when he was Brigade Major. General Alexander then invited them to stay at his headquarters, and here they met General Eisenhower. In a few days they were flown home to Scotland.

O'Connor was delighted to be given command of a corps under Field Marshal Montgomery in the invasion of Europe. But he never forgot the years in Italy and after the war was over he made annual visits with his wife to seek out and thank again those Italians who had helped in his escape at the risk of their own lives.

The story of General O'Connor and his companions is only one of many, mostly unrecorded, in which Anglo-Italian, and more especially Anglo-Tuscan, friendship was severely tried and proven. In *Rossano*, published in 1955, Gordon Lett wrote an absorbing account of escape and resistance in the Apennines and in the Carrara area. As a British major he took charge of and trained a sizeable troop of partisans who attacked German camps and sabotaged installations, always shaking off pursuit and returning by devious routes to their mountain hide-out. Eric Newby in 1971 published his story of *Love and War in the Apennines*, dedicated 'To all those Italians who helped me, and thousands like me, at the risk of their lives . . .' His story had a happy ending, for he went back and married the young Italian with whom he had fallen in love when they shared the dangers and hunger. Since then they have spent part of every year in their house in Tuscany.

Thirty years after the war ended the Mayor of Bagni di Lucca, Enzo Tintori, welcomed a conference headed by the British Ambassador in Rome, Sir Guy Millard, and organized by Ian Greenlees, director of the British Institute in Florence, on 'Italy and Great Britain in the Struggle for Liberation'.[5] Those who lectured, both Italian and British, contributed fascinating recollections of the final struggle to free Italy from Fascism and from the German occupation. As the letter read to the conference from the Vice President of the European Commission, the then Sir Christopher Soames, put it,

> . . . there were on the day of the Armistice some 75,000 prisoners-of-war in prison camps in Italy. The fact that some 50,000 of them managed to avoid recapture and to find their way back to the Allied lines is a remarkable tribute to the gallantry of countless Italians who helped them on their way.

[5] Proceedings published as *Italia e Gran Bretagna nella Lotta di Liberazione*, La Nuova Italia. Editrice Firenze (1977).

A more practical tribute to this gallantry, however, was the Boys' Town established at Modena after an appeal which General O'Connor helped to sponsor in 1950. The appeal had a Foreword by Field Marshal Viscount Alexander of Tunis, who wrote: 'I can think of no better way to show our gratitude than by making our contribution towards the erection of a Community Centre for the orphans of Italians killed in Italy during the war as a result of their activities in helping our countrymen.' The *Città dei Ragazzi* or Boys' Town is now a thriving establishment; some of the boys come over for a few weeks every year on a visit to British homes, and many enduring friendships have started from this.

Select Bibliography

My *Paradise of Exiles* (1974) includes a list of guidebooks and maps of Tuscany, as well as a full bibliography—in effect a catalogue of my own Anglo–Tuscan library. Much of the background reading listed there is of equal relevance to the present book, and my library has been enlarged to include many of the sources drawn on for this book and acknowledged in the text. The following list does not pretend to be comprehensive, but includes a selection of recent books (a few in Italian) on the places and some of the people dealt with here which may be of interest to the general reader.

On the historical background, and Tuscany past and present:
M. S. Anderson, *Europe in the Eighteenth Century* (1961)
George Blake, *The Ben Line* (1956)
Arthur Bryant, *The Medieval Foundation* (1966)
Luciano Casella, *I cavatori delle Alpi Apuane* (Carrara, 1963)
Eric Cochrane, *Florence in the Forgotten Centuries 1527–1800* (1973)
Alec Glasfurd, *Siena and the Hill Towns* (1962)
Michael Grant, *The World of Rome* (1960)
Gordon Lett, *Rossano: An Adventure of the Italian Resistance* (1955)
R. J. Mitchell, *The Laurels and the Tiara: Pope Pius II* (1962)
Brian Moloney, *Florence and England: Essays on Cultural Relations in the Second Half of the Eighteenth Century* (Firenze, 1969)
Eric Newby, *Love and War in the Apennines* (1971)
Cesare Sardi, *Vita lucchese nel Settecento* (Lucca, 1968)
A. Lytton Sells, *The Paradise of Travellers* (1964)
Maurice Vaussard, *Daily Life in Eighteenth Century Italy* (1962)

On the Stuart connection:
Bryan Bevan, *I Was James II's Queen* (1963)
   King James the Third of England (1967)

Margaret Crosland, *Louise of Stolberg* (1962)
David Daiches, *Charles Edward Stuart* (1973)
Margaret Forster, *The Rash Adventurer: The Rise and Fall of Charles Edward Stuart* (1973)
Mary Hopkirk, *Queen Over the Water: Mary of Modena* (1953)
Carola Oman, *Mary of Modena* (1975)
Baron Porcelli, *The White Cockade: The Lives and Adventurers of James Francis Edward Stuart and His Sons . . .* (1949)
Henrietta Tayler, *Prince Charlie's Daughter* (1950)

On artists, art historians and collectors:

Harold Acton, *More Memoirs of an Aesthete* (1970)
Bernard Berenson, *Rumour and Reflection* (1952)
　The Passionate Sightseer (1960)
　Sunset and Twilight (1964)
　The Making of a Connoisseur (1979)
Kenneth Clark, *Another Part of the Wood: A Self-Portrait* (1974)
C. L. Dentler, *Famous Foreigners in Florence* (1964)
John Fleming, *Robert Adam and His Circle* (1962)
Brian Fothergill, *Sir William Hamilton* (1969)
Adeline Hartcup, *Angelica* (1954)
James Lees-Milne, *The Age of Adam* (1947)
Derrick Leon, *Ruskin the Great Victorian* (1949)
Nicky Mariano, *Forty Years with Bernard Berenson* (1966)
Dorothy Moulton Mayer, *Angelica Kauffmann R.A.* (1972)
O. Millar, *Zoffany and His Tribune* (1967)
Alan Moorehead, *A Late Education* (1970)
Mario Praz, *Conversation Pieces* (1971)
Peter Quennell, *Ruskin* (1963)
John D. Rosenberg, *The Darkening Glass: A Portrait of Ruskin's Genius* (1961)
Maryle Secrest, *Being Bernard Berenson* (1979)
Harold I. Shapiro, *Ruskin in Italy* (1972)
Sylvia Sprigge, *Berenson* (1960)
Francis Henry Taylor, *The Taste of Angels: A History of Art Collecting from Rameses to Napoleon* (1949)
John Walker, *Self-Portrait with Donors* (1969)

INDEX

A figure 2 in brackets immediately after a page reference indicates that there are two separate references to the subject on that page.

Index

Index